Oneness

Torn Curtain Publishing
Wellington, New Zealand
www.torncurtainpublishing.com

© Copyright 2022 Bob Cheesman. All rights reserved.

ISBN Softcover 978-0-473-66006-2
ISBN EPub 978-0-473-66007-9

No portion of this book may be reproduced, stored in a retrieval system or transmitted in any form or by any means—electronic, mechanical, photocopy, recording or otherwise—except for brief quotations in printed reviews or promotion, without prior written permission from the author.

Unless otherwise indicated, all Scripture quotations are taken from the Holy Bible, New Living Translation, copyright © 1996, 2004, 2015 by Tyndale House Foundation. Used by permission of Tyndale House Publishers, Carol Stream, Illinois 60188. All rights reserved.

Scripture quotations marked NIV are taken from the Holy Bible, New International Version©, NIV©. Copyright ©1973, 1978, 1984, 2011 by Biblica, Inc.© Used by permission of Zondervan. All rights reserved worldwide.

Scripture quotations marked ESV are from The ESV© Bible (The Holy Bible, English Standard Version©), copyright © 2001 by Crossway, a publishing ministry of Good News Publishers. Used by permission. All rights reserved.

Cover photography by Amy Dekker. Used with permission.

Cataloguing in Publishing Data
Title: Oneness: Experiencing God's Design for Marriage
Author: Bob Cheesman
Subjects: Christian living, dating and marriage, family relationships

A copy of this title is held at the National Library of New Zealand.

Oneness

Experiencing God's Design
for Marriage

BOB CHEESMAN

This book is dedicated to Mary who has been my partner for fifty-six years and who I dearly love more today than ever. Thank you, Mary.

Love as distinct from 'being in love' is not merely a feeling. It is a deep unity, maintained by the will and deliberately strengthened by habit; reinforced by the grace which both partners ask, and receive, from God.

They can have this love for each other even at those moments when they do not like each other; as you love yourself even when you do not like yourself.

— C. S. Lewis

Contents

Introduction		*1*
Part One: God's Design for Marriage		*5*
Chapter 1	What is Godly Marriage?	7
Chapter 2	A Partnership of Equals	18
Chapter 3	Understanding One Another	28
Part Two: Before you Embark on Marriage		*37*
Chapter 4	Choose Wisely	39
Chapter 5	The Battle of the Outlaws	49
Chapter 6	Daily Life	57
Part Three: Foundations for a Healthy Marriage		*65*
Chapter 7	Intercommunication	67
Chapter 8	Intimacy	75
Chapter 9	Money	86
Chapter 10	Faith	96
Part Four: After the Wedding		*105*
Chapter 11	Marriage Check-up	107
Chapter 12	Then Came the Children	114
Chapter 13	What if it Goes Wrong?	121
Epilogue		*129*
Appendix: Marriage Health Indicator		*135*
Recommended Ministries and Resources		*143*
Acknowledgements		*145*

Introduction

It is 1956; I am sixteen years old and about to leave boarding school and go into a world of which I know little. Since the age of four or five, I have been in the care of Shaftesbury Homes, England, only making the occasional visit home during holidays. I have little or no memory of living at home with my father and stepmother, and as for my birth mother, her identity and whereabouts are unknown to me—it will be another two years before I meet her. I have no idea about money, have never cooked my own meals nor done my own laundry, and using a telephone is a mystery to me. In short, my upbringing has left me ill-equipped for the world I am being sent into.

For the first three or four years after leaving school I will live in hostels, and eventually, a bedsit, while working with a film company as a messenger boy. In time, they will train me to be a rostrum cameraman. But I am largely isolated and alone, with little or no experience of what it means to belong to a family. I have had no demonstration—good or bad—of being married, and absolutely no idea about children and parenting. I also have no idea about girls. My school was an all-boys one, full of gutter-talk but little reality. Yet marriage and parenting will become the very things I will develop a passion for.

~

My first memory of meeting my wife, Mary, who was my sister's best friend, was on a church day trip to the coast to which I had been invited. She was actually there with another boy, but I was attracted to her and she obviously to me, because we later started dating. There was, however, a big problem in that Mary was a Christian, and I was not. Furthermore,

I had no intention of getting involved with God or church. It was not that I was resolutely set against either; it was just that at boarding school we'd had to go to church five, sometimes even six, days a week. We had no choice in the matter. Attending services was compulsory for all students, and consequently, I did not wish to ever return to church.

Mary and I have different stories as to how our brief relationship ended. She says she gave me up because I was not a Christian, and I say that it was me who gave her up because she was a religious maniac! However, on the day we stopped going out, I had a rather strange experience while I was waiting at the bus stop to go home. It was late evening, and the bus stop was located in the middle of a council housing estate with large blocks of flats. That night, it was completely deserted. Then suddenly, I heard a man's voice say very loudly, "You will marry that girl!"

To say I was shocked would be an understatement. I looked around, but there was no other person in sight. Being me, I just shrugged and got on the bus when it came a few minutes later. Mary was sixteen, and I was nineteen or twenty.

Even though Mary and I were no longer an 'item' as they say, I still kept in touch with her family, and some five years later, when I was twenty-four, her parents asked me to take Mary to a Christian camp reunion because they did not want her to go on the train on her own. I said I would not go on the train, but offered to take her on my motorcycle. Somehow, they agreed to this arrangement—I think principally because they knew I would be exposed to the gospel if they could get me to that reunion. Well, they were right. That event did expose me to the gospel, and eventually I did become a Christian—but not before an epic mental battle and some considerable rebellion on my part.

It was during this time that Mary's mum sent me a letter telling me that I was breaking Mary's heart, and I should either get in, or get out. With this ultimatum, I decided to give church a go for a while, believing that within a few weeks I would prove it all nonsense and be free to go back to my usual life. How wrong I was! I soon accepted Christ, was baptised and filled with the Holy Spirit, and within seven years was made the pastor of Bermondsey Elim church. (This is not as grand as it sounds—the church had twelve people, only two of whom were under sixty, and I was still working full-time in the film industry!)

Now that I was an active Christian, Mary and I started dating again, and eventually, in March 1966, we married. As I write this, we have been married for fifty-five years. Whenever we tell people we have been together all those years, there are exclamations of, "Wow, that's great!" Yet for the first ten years or so it was not great, to say the least, and were it not for our faith, we might never have made it this far.

Why was it so bad? The short answer is this: We were both—especially me—ignorant of how to relate as husband and wife. Somebody once told me that my problem was that I was looking for Mary to be my mother, rather than my wife. That insight spoke to me more than anything else, and I realised it was true. Because I never had a mother, I was subconsciously longing for a mother-figure in my life. This had a profound effect on how I viewed and related to Mary. Mary, on the other hand, had been brought up in a good Christian home with two parents who loved her immensely. However, there was little, if any, physical affection on display either between her mum and dad, or toward or among the three children. In addition to this, they had strict rules about many things relating to the outworking of their faith, including Sunday observance.

So, take a man who had no example, teaching, or experience of how to relate to the opposite sex, and a woman who had been brought up with little physical affection and a fair degree of legalism but plenty of love, put them together with no help, and because they are Christians, expect them to be able to relate well and form a good marriage partnership, and you have a recipe for trouble. We were, for several years, deeply unhappy. We had different priorities. We also had different ideas about physical affection, about how we should manage our money, and about parenting. We had no idea how to put things right and thought we were simply incompatible. The truth is that we were ignorant; we simply had no idea how to relate to each other.

What changed? As church leaders, Mary and I were faced with married couples coming to us wanting help with marriage problems, as well as those getting married wanting some pre-marriage preparation. The question for us was, *How were we going to do that when we were not exactly doing well in our own marriage?* We had to learn and learn fast as we were not prepared to be hypocrites. We studied what the Bible had to say and read books on the subject. The more we learned the more our relationship improved, until one day, we found ourselves in a sound, loving, and fulfilled marriage. Not to say that we never had any problems ever again—we did, but the difference was we now knew how to bring ourselves out of those problems and back into that loving, committed relationship.

During our years of ministry we have had the privilege of taking engaged couples through marriage preparation classes. The material we used has evolved over the years, and the thought occurred that I should write down this teaching so that it might continue to help people in the future. We have also used similar material to help couples who found themselves in difficulty—and although not every marriage was able to be salvaged, many were.

This book is the result of a journey of discovery that took place over the course of many years, which we now want to pass on to everyone willing to read it. It is designed to help prepare those who are engaged for marriage, and to enable those who are already married to refresh their marriages and straighten out paths that are hindering rather than helping. We hope that these things will become embedded into your lives so that relating well to your partner becomes natural and instinctive for you. It is, above all, the story of God's design for a successful joining of a man and woman in marriage. Go God's way and not the way of the world and you will find life as God intended it to be.

—Bob Cheesman

PART ONE

God's Design for Marriage

1

What is Godly Marriage?

A Sunday School teacher once asked her students if there were any prayer needs. A little girl asked if they could pray for her, because as of Saturday, she was going to have a new father. It turned out her mother and her mother's boyfriend (let's call them Jane and Henry), who were Christians and members of our church, had decided to move in together. This very innocent prayer request presented a problem for both Henry and Jane, and for the church. The dilemma was this: *Was it okay for two of God's people to just move in together, and what constitutes marriage for those who profess to follow God's ways and precepts?*

This situation resulted in conflict between the couple and the church of which I was a leader at the time. And so, I and another leader went to talk with Henry about what we considered a godly way to approach the next step in their relationship. Unfortunately, Jane was ill so we were unable to include her in the conversation, but we put the question to him: *Was moving in together the correct way forward for them before God?*

Being a new Christian, Henry was angry with what he saw as our interference in their private affairs. He had no concept of what marriage from a biblical perspective was, nor, apparently, of what it meant to be a church member. He simply saw what his friends and acquaintances were doing and decided the same approach would work in his relationship with Jane. As far as he was concerned, this had nothing to do with anyone else—not the church, or the church leaders. His anger was such that he and Jane left the church and moved in together.

From the church's perspective, we were left trying to find the balance between our responsibility as leaders to guide our people in the ways of God according to what we saw the Bible as teaching, with our belief in (and value for) personal responsibility. We couldn't dictate how church members should live. But of course, the question then arises, *Do we accept that 'anything goes' within church life?* The answer must be no—which brings us to the choice Henry and Jane faced: to remain accountable within the fellowship of believers, or to leave and go their own way.

But there were further questions that arose out of this situation, questions that are still relevant today, like:

What is marriage?

Is marriage necessary?

Why should Christian couples like Henry and Jane not choose to just move in and live together?

As Christians, we work out our choices before God, seeking to live according to his will as revealed through the Bible, God's Word, which we believe to be authoritative. This applies to every aspect of our lives, and therefore we cannot leave our relationships out. To answer these questions well, we need to explore what it means to live together in the context of following God.

DEFINING MARRIAGE

Historically, marriages were primarily about alliances between families. Protection, safety, procreation, the continuance of the family name and wellbeing, and the strengthening of future trade were the main considerations when parents were considering a marriage. The selection of a life partner had little to do with the couple themselves. But over time, as global economies developed, all this became less important, and the subsequent changes in society allowed a greater awareness of the feelings of the people getting married. Eventually, it became almost entirely about personal choice. The concepts of initial attraction, followed by love, were placed at the forefront of the decision of who to spend your life with—so much so that these have now become the driving force of marriage, at least in the 'western world'.

Over my own lifetime, much about marriage has continued to change. When Mary and I got married, there was little difference between our approach as Christians to dating, getting engaged, planning the wedding, and going on a honeymoon, and any other marriage taking place between non-Christians in the local registrar office or in a church building. This is because at that time, marriage within the wider culture was based on Christian values and biblical concepts. A necessary precursor to a lifelong partnership, marriage was seen as being between a man and a woman who joined together to form a new relationship by the making of covenantal promises to one another before witnesses in a public ceremony. After this, a marriage certificate was issued; it was a legal document that registered the marriage in the law of the country.

Today, the order of events has largely been reversed. People generally date, then move in together, have children, and get married later—or they may never get married. Cohabitation without the legal commitment of marriage—both between men and women, or those of the same sex—has become the norm. These developments have resulted in a marked contrast between the way the non-Christian world and faith communities go about establishing new relationships. They have also influenced how many Christians approach their life partnerships.

In discussing these things with a church leader, I was told that in some churches cohabitation has become so widespread that leaders are no longer addressing the issue, and living together outside of the marriage covenant is in danger of becoming acceptable, even within the church, regardless of what the Bible teaches.

It is easy, and sometimes convenient, to just flow with what is happening in wider society. Yet, as Christians, we need to seek out God's will for marriage and have the conviction to carry through on our conclusions.

This leads us to the important question regarding the nature of 'cohabitation'. *Is it marriage or not?* The term and the concept, which although considered a fairly recent phenomenon, have been used since the 1500s to refer to a couple living together without being married. One dictionary defines it as, 'To live together as if married, usually without legal or religious sanction; to live together in an intimate relationship; to live together as husband and wife especially without being married'.

While couples who live together without a ceremony are not considered legally married because they lack a signed marriage certificate as proof of their union, in New Zealand a cohabitating couple is now considered to be in a common-law marriage, or, in legal terms, a de-facto relationship, after they have been together for three years or when they have a child together. When couples in these types of relationships separate, children, property and other assets are treated in the same way as if the couple were lawfully married and in possession of a marriage certificate.

These changes mean that 'marriage' is no longer solely defined by the State as being in possession of a piece of paper, but also by the length of time a couple have been cohabiting, and whether or not they have children. Given this situation, do we, as Christians, still need a legal marriage certificate to be considered married in God's eyes? If not, what are the implications?

Answering these questions compels us to define the parameters of Christian marriage. To do so, we must base our concepts and actions on Scripture, rather than personal opinion or what is convenient. Just because something is the norm in the non-Christian world does not mean it is right for God's people.

MARRIAGE VERSUS COHABITATION

The first mention of a topic in Scripture is always a good place to start if we want to discover what God has to say about something. In this case, the first reference to marriage is found right at the beginning of the Bible, in Genesis, where God created what is termed 'man' (Genesis 1:27). It's important that we understand that this reference to 'man' is not exclusively male; it is a generic term that encompasses both male and female. In other words, mankind is not made up of two essentially different species, but rather one human species, represented through both male and female.

What we see in the first two chapters of Genesis is the bringing together of Adam and Eve, male and female, in a permanent partnership, thus establishing the principle of marriage. The male was created first and the female was created from him, and the way that God brought about the joining (or 'oneness') between them was to establish a deep magnetic attraction in the male toward his female counterpart. When the male first met her, it was a *'wow'* moment, a moment when time stopped for him.

Before the other half of humanity was revealed to Adam, every animal had passed by and had no such effect upon him—there was no allure, no fundamental connection. He named each species, yet was drawn toward none of them. But when he saw Eve, the female of his own species and the counterpart of him, his response was, "This is it, this is the one!" In that instant, a deep-seated attraction was born in the male toward the female. That attraction has never changed; it is still there. This was not lust, but a pull toward her that resulted in devotion and the desire to be together, to work together, live together, and to form a partnership. Adam's words reflect this idea of being part of one another: "This is now bone of my bones and flesh of my flesh; she shall be called 'woman', for she was taken out of man" (Genesis 2:23, NIV). What he means is, "Wow, she is mine, part of me, and I cannot live without her. I will leave everything I know to be with her!"

We know that you cannot base a relationship solely on attraction. Although that is often the starting point, it will never be enough to sustain a relationship; at some point, chemistry must give way to commitment. And of course, not all relationships start with physical attraction. Some are looking for the will of God and praying for a godly partner in life, somebody God has chosen for them. If that, is you, watch out because God surprises us when we seek his will, and we do not always get what we expect! This was certainly the case for a friend of ours. He was a pastor, and whenever he saw us, he posed the question, "When is God going to give me a wife?" Eventually we asked what he was looking for, and when he described his ideal woman—very attractive, slim, black silky dress, high heels, a good hairstyle, very trendy—we had a good chuckle and told him we were not surprised that God had left him single!

One day, a member of our friend's congregation, who was very needy, turned up at our church. We met with her and subsequently got in touch with our friend, suggesting he meet with her and try to help her. We also suggested he find a mature woman who he could trust to join him for these meetings. As it turns out, there was a lady in his church who was very well thought of. The matron of a care home, she was the opposite to the description of his ideal woman, but she had a beautiful personality and was well-liked by everybody. After the two of them met with the young woman they were trying to help, they would go for a coffee together to discuss how they were getting on. Over time, they discovered a growing attraction to one another. Then God spoke to our friend, "This is the one you have been asking for." And the rest is history!

From the moment Adam saw Eve, it signalled a future where men would experience such a strong attraction that they would want to leave home to be joined with a female. This, then, is the underpinning principle of godly, and therefore, Christian, marriage: A man will leave his childhood home, his father and mother, his brothers and sisters, all he has known to be united to his wife and they will become one flesh (Genesis 2:24). The attraction is strong, mutual, never one-sided, and as it grows, it creates a desire in them both to be together permanently. This leads them to commit to becoming husband and wife in a binding marriage covenant made before God, family, and friends. Their physical and sexual union is the ultimate fulfilment of this covenant, the result of a deep mutual commitment to each other whereby 'two become one'.

WHAT IS GODLY MARRIAGE?

Before I was married, I remember listening to a man describe this phenomenon. He had met a girl and had completely fallen for her. He hated to be apart from her and used to travel 140 miles on his motorcycle every weekend to be with her and then travel back ready to start work on Monday. He married her and remained completely devoted to her all her life. I remember being slightly baffled by his attraction to one girl. I liked girls and was attracted to the female form but had not experienced this attraction to one singular female—until I met Mary. Then I understood. Even after being together for fifty-five years, I still love her and continue to be attracted and devoted to her.

I saw this vividly again around three years ago. A friend rang me and asked if we could have coffee as he wanted to chat. What he really wanted was to share with me that he had met a girl on a blind date. He was smitten. They had talked and talked, shared about themselves, and found an instant attraction toward each other. This was so much more than a physical or sexual attraction; it was a deeply emotional magnetic attraction that drew these two people together. My friend wanted advice on how to go forward and explore this potential relationship. This couple have now been married for two years, and recently I asked his wife, "How's married life?" Her face lit up as she replied, "Wonderful! Best thing I ever did." Later I asked her husband the same question; when he looked over at her, you could see the answer in the way he looked at his wife, and then he expressed the same feelings toward her. They dated, got married, set up a home together, and now they have a delightful baby boy.

∼

We have established attraction as the catalyst for marital relationships, yet the question remains: *At what point, in God's eyes, are a couple finally considered married?* The straightforward answer is: when they become 'one flesh'. In other words, when they have sex for the first time. When Isaac married Rebekah, we are simply told that he took her into his mother's tent (Genesis 24:67). His mother had died, so he was not taking her in to introduce her to his mother! Rather, the implication is that this is when they became 'one' and were considered married. This is the straightforward understanding of 'leaving and cleaving' (Genesis 2:24). Rebekah had been chosen by God to be Isaac's wife. Little else is said about the initiation and conventions of their marriage. It's a bare-bones story, but from the moment Isaac took his wife into his tent and they were physically united, they were considered 'one'.

I have recently been reading about the history of the Native American Sioux people. A man would court a woman he was attracted to. Interestingly, if she responded, she would eventually take him into her tepee, have sex with him, and the whole tribe then considered them married.

In the United Kingdom, before the marriage act of 1753, 'banns' (old English for a 'proclamation') had to be published and displayed publicly, then a marriage ceremony performed by a Church of England minister. Every marriage had to be consummated by sexual intercourse, and without this, a marriage could be declared invalid and annulled. There was no centralised record of marriages, yet once you had gone through this process you were considered married and needed to divorce in a court of law if you wished to separate. The point I make is that the cultural conventions of the society in which we live dictate the principles that hold marriages together and make them legally binding.

According to the conventions of the United Kingdom where we were married, and New Zealand where we now live, you are considered married if you have been through a marriage ceremony before family and friends and have signed the marriage register and are therefore in possession of a marriage certificate. The fundamental difference between the Christian and non-Christian, is that the non-Christian sees nothing wrong with cohabitation and having children together prior to that marriage ceremony, whereas the Christian belief is that the public declaration of vows at the wedding ceremony marks the start of married life together, and that the period leading up to that point is preparation for this lifetime commitment. Until that moment, cohabitation is not an option for the believer.

WHAT IS GODLY MARRIAGE?

The reason for this difference is the Bible's teaching that sex is solely intended within the confines of marriage, and is a sacred, covenantal act of commitment. Numerous times in Scripture we are told to avoid even a hint of sexual immorality, because this is " improper for God's holy people" (Ephesians 5:3-4, NIV). Of course, we need to know what the Bible means by 'sexual immorality'. From Paul's letter to the Corinthian church, we see that it refers to sexual activity, in all of its various forms, outside of a marriage relationship. The Corinthians had written to Paul with some questions on which they wanted clarification, and while we don't have the specific questions, only the answers that Paul gave them, what is evident is that they were having issues with sexual activity in the church.

Paul begins his answer by stating his personal opinion that it is good for people to stay unmarried. However, he goes on to say that because there was so much sexual immorality among them, they ought to marry (1 Corinthians 7:8-9). It seems clear that these believers were choosing not to marry—possibly because of Paul's previous teaching that it was better not to—but still having sex. In response, Paul tells the Corinthian Christians that rather than having 'casual sex', they should get married so that each person could satisfy the sexual needs they were experiencing without engaging in immoral practices. He reaffirms this position in his letter to the Thessalonians, where he states, "It is God's will that you should be sanctified: that you should avoid sexual immorality; that each of you should learn to control his own body in a way that is holy and honourable, not in passionate lust like the heathen, who do not know God" (1 Thessalonians 4:3-6, NIV).

Why is it wrong to have sex if you are not married? I will attempt to give an answer, but bear in mind that it is enough that we trust God and obey what he says, even if we do not fully understand why. Personal conviction is important, and each of us need to conduct ourselves according to our own consciences in the light of biblical revelation. But even if we do not understand why God says sex should be exclusive to marriage, we still have to ask ourselves who we are following—God, or the world? When

Peter reacted to Jesus telling the disciples that he was going to be killed, he said, "That will never happen to you!" In reply, Jesus said, "You do not have in mind the concerns of God, but merely human concerns" (Matthew 16:23, NIV). As believers, we must set out hearts on doing things God's way. How we conduct our relationships is important to God, and he wants us to understand the value of the covenant of marriage where two become one spiritually, mentally, and physically through the joining of their bodies.

Sexual union for God's people is covenantal. This is the reason that sexual union with somebody outside of marriage is such a big 'no-no'; it breaks the intimate covenantal commitment, and is why Jesus taught that divorce is permissible (Matthew 5:32). In Malachi 2, a passage of Scripture we will return to many times, God reminds his people that *he is the witness between them and the wife of their youth, the wife of their marriage covenant* (vv.13-14). A godly marriage, therefore, is when two people commit themselves to form a partnership together through making life-long, public promises of commitment to each other before God. They then become one flesh through sex after that ceremonial joining, so fulfilling God's design for intimacy.

It could be deduced that, if having sex together is the point where God considers the two to have become one, it is alright to move in together as Henry and Jane did, and skip the wedding ceremony altogether. The problem with this view, however, is that, for God's people, there has always been a definite moment of commitment when promises are made to one another. What is more, those promises, made publicly before God himself, and before family and friends, and are a covenant for life. This is not something to be taken lightly, but seriously, and with the intention of a lifelong commitment toward one another.

∼

What happened to Henry and Jane? Two years after they left the church, we received a phone call asking if they could return, as they had now gotten married. Because there had been a significant and difficult rift between us, we knew that there first needed to be reconciliation between them and us as a leadership, so we arranged for a meeting. They told us they had missed our church because in the end it was their home, and they wanted to return. When we asked about the conflict surrounding their decision to move in together, Henry shared with us that a deep conviction had come over him that he had got it badly wrong and that what they did was not right before God. It was with great pleasure that we were able to welcome them back into fellowship and celebrate their new marriage.

2

A Partnership of Equals

I had recently begun pastoring a new church and had been reviewing the Sunday School teaching teams when I suggested that Tom and Betty form a new team. They both were agreeable to this, so I was somewhat shocked when Tom immediately announced to everyone that as he was the man, he would be the leader in this new teaching partnership. Behind his statement was generations of teaching that women were created to serve men. Indeed, there is one denomination whose constitution states this position as fact: *Women were created to serve men.* It's a line of thinking that runs throughout Christianity, and is the reason many brides have either chosen or been required to say the word 'obey' when making their marriage vows.

I want to put before you that it is not a matter of who is the 'top dog' between the male and female in a marriage relationship, or indeed between men and women in general. It is a matter of equality. God did not design one sex to subjugate the other but for us to complement each other and work alongside one another as equal partners. However, the problem many believers have with the concept of equality between husbands and wives is that the words the English Bible uses to describe their relationship seem to paint the very opposite picture to equality—words like, 'lord', 'a helper' and 'submit'. Add to these the fact that men are termed the 'head' in the marriage relationship (Ephesians 5:23), and we can be forgiven for conjuring up a picture of female inferiority. In fact, many would tell you that they wish the Bible did not use this terminology at all. Life would be much easier if we were to ignore these specific words of scripture and just live our lives with love and respect for each other. *Is there, then, any value in retaining what seems to many to be an archaic view of married life?* The answer is *yes*.

If we desire to follow God's blueprint for our marriages and relationships, we cannot ignore these words; rather, we need to understand why they are in the Bible, what they mean, and what they teach us about how God has made men and women and the roles and giftings he has called us to. Let's begin this exploration by turning to God's original intentions in creation before corruption entered and the human race was separated from God.

THE REALITY OF A FALLEN WORLD

Genesis chapter one starts with God creating mankind, and portrays them as having a strong sense of unity and partnership (Genesis 1:26-27). The principle is that he created mankind in his likeness, male and female, to look after his creation. Vine's Expository Dictionary explains the Hebrew word for 'likeness' as: 'To be or act like, resemble, compare, devise, balance, or ponder'. To reflect on this is to conclude that both sexes together, male and female, represent God's person and values. This newly-created partnership was given the task of living in and taking care of the planet God had created; that is, looking after the world's resources. They were to do this *together*. It is a picture of partnership, intimacy and unity through which the world would be populated and taken care of.

Unity, however, does not mean conformity of role or purpose—this is something we see when we look at the details of creation in Genesis chapter two. God formed Adam from the dust and placed him in the garden to work it and take care of it (Genesis 2:15). After giving him instructions, God declared that it was not good for Adam to be alone in this task; he needed help, a partner to share the responsibility with him. But in all the animal kingdom there was no suitable partner for him (Genesis 2:20). The word translated as 'suitable' tells us much about what ensues. It means 'in front of' or, 'before your face', and carries the meaning of 'corresponding to' or 'parallel to something that is standing alongside'. This indicates that for Adam there was no match for him in the animal kingdom, nobody who could stand with him as a partner to help him.

In standard English, the word 'helper' indicates a subservient position; it refers to an 'assistant' or 'a person who gives support'. However, a more true perspective includes the one being helped. Looking at it from this angle, it carried the idea of somebody who 'stands before you', someone who is 'a part of you or parallel to you, someone who is on the same level'—not someone who is inferior to you. In fact, the Hebrew word *ezer* (used for 'helper' in the creation narrative) is used twenty-one times in the Old Testament, primarily in relation to God helping mankind. As the Psalmist proclaims, "My help comes from the Lord" (Psalm 121:2). The *help* that the woman offers man is the same help that God offers his people. It is a strong, collaborative word—a word of power. The animal kingdom was below Adam; there was no equal there for him, nobody who could stand alongside him. So God created Eve to be his partner to stand with him in stewarding God's creation and fulfilling his command to subdue and fill the earth.

This portrays a story of order and purpose, but also of equality and harmony. At creation, there would have been no cause to protest at injustice, abuse, or domination. But this harmony was spoilt when mankind became increasingly independent of God and sought to do things their own way. Genesis 3 makes it clear to us that there were consequences for walking away from God—consequences that both men and women have had to live with ever since.

For woman, her pain in childbirth would increase, and rather than reigning alongside her husband, he would rule over her (Genesis 3:16). The curse of sin, of mankind turning their backs on God and his established order, marks the beginning of men's dominance over women in a way that distresses the heart of God and was never part of his original design.

Even so, a deep longing would persist within women to find a husband—a desire that appears to remain strong, considering one of the most popular genres of film and literature continues to be romance, where the storylines revolve around a man and a woman finding and falling in love with one another.

For man, the consequences of the Fall were that providing food for his family would become hard, and the elements would conspire against him—it would only be by the sweat of his face that he would eat bread (Genesis 3:17-19). Life from this point on would be very different from what God had intended, and consequently, people would seek to find their security in many other things, including relationships outside of marriage.

Our modern world may feel far removed from these events, but we can still trace the Genesis-story in the way we desire to live, and the ongoing consequences we endure as a result of the effects of the Fall. The truth is that the interrelationship between men and women is the foundation on which we continue to build our society, and there remains a deep yearning for intimacy and for the security of belonging. Yet we also find men abusing and dominating women, and families struggling to put food on the table. We want change. We want our relationships to succeed and to be what God intended them to be, but divorce rates and the number of wives who end up in refuges tell us that we are falling very short of what we desire.

While the threads of creation's story might largely be lost on the non-believer, for us it brings understanding amid a fallen world. It also brings us to the question: *As Christians, how should our experience of marriage be different to that of the world?* To answer this, we must look to Jesus.

The coming of Jesus changed everything, because being in Christ has the potential to return us to what God intended for us from the outset. For this to be our reality, however, we must be willing to embrace the full teaching of redemption. To be 'redeemed' is to be brought back from being lost and separated from God and to be restored to our original status as children of God. While we still live within a fallen world, Christ has rescued us from the darkness that befell the human race and transferred us back to God's Kingdom (Colossians 1:13-14).

This redemption-story must be reflected in the marriage relationship between godly men and women.

THE REDEEMED ORDER

Although the words 'submit' and 'headship' remain in Scripture, their meaning takes on a new dimension when we understand redemption. The apostle Paul set out the pattern for how husbands and wives are to relate to one another in Ephesians chapter five. For wives, the instruction is straightforward—they are to submit to their husbands (Ephesians 5:22-23). The word 'submit' is not in the original Greek text, which reads, "wives unto your husbands as to the Lord." But even though the word itself is not present, the implication is clear in the statement, "as to the Lord." Two verses later, when Paul sums up his point, he explicitly uses the word 'submit' concerning how the church is to relate to Christ: "As the church submits to Christ, so you wives should submit to your husbands in everything" (Ephesians 5:24).

Jesus is Lord, so we place ourselves under him. We do so because we know that he loves us, and we in turn, love him and are committed to him in every way. You could also say that he is more powerful than we are so it would be crazy to reverse the order of submission.

Interestingly, in these verses Paul simply stated Roman law which required women to submit to and obey their husbands. He could have gone up against the law, but he chose to instruct wives to comply with the law as it was at the time of his writing. What was revolutionary however, were his instructions for how husbands were to respond to their wives' submission. Unlike his directions to wives, in his instructions to husbands, Paul went against what would have been the prevailing view, teaching them to behave in a way that, in a Roman context, is nothing short of dynamite!

Continuing with the analogy of the church and Christ concerning how husbands should treat their wives, Paul explains that the husband is the 'head' of the wife just as Christ is the head of the church (v. 23). There is no mistaking this word—it means 'head' as in 'one who is responsible for something or somebody'. However, that he is the head is a statement, not an instruction. In other words, the man is never told that he is the boss and can order his wife around or dominate her in any way he wishes. In fact, nowhere in this passage is a husband ever told by Paul to rule over his wife. On the contrary, he is given an example of how to fulfil his headship—and it is not domination. The example he is given is the way Christ gave himself up for the Church. Christ sacrificed everything for her—his very life, even. The instruction on how a husband is to fulfil his headship is to *love his wife as Christ loved the church and gave himself up for her* (Ephesians 5:25). That is revolutionary! Rather than rule or dominate, he is to give himself up. In other words, he must put his wife first.

Finally, all this is summed up in the last verse of the passage. Husbands are to love their wives as themselves, and wives are to respect their husbands (Ephesians 5:33). The physically stronger male is told to give himself to the welfare of his physically weaker female—not mentally or giftedly weaker, just physically. *Why?* Because God is looking for a partnership of equals who together live before him in harmony, peace, and safety.

∼

Having established in principle how God designed us to relate to one another, it is left to consider how these concepts of headship and submission play out in daily life. Do wives who are committed to God go around constantly thinking, *I must submit to my husband,* or do husbands repeat to themselves, *I must remember that I am the head in this relationship*? No married couple I know goes about life with such thoughts. Indeed, if a couple did seek to practice God's will in such a way, they would immediately find themselves entrenched in legalism.

As we seek to model our marriages on God's design, we have a choice to reduce our partnership to obeying a set of rules or to embrace the power of grace. Law always results in inflexibility which in turn leads to living with failure as we quickly discover we cannot possibly live up to God's standards. Legalism would take the words 'submit' and 'head' and interpret them literally, requiring wives to submit to and obey their husbands in everything. Indeed it has, for generations, been interpreted in this way, and consequently, many husbands have dominated their wives in a way God never intended.

Under grace we understand that headship looks very different, because true grace will always see headship as the responsibility to bestow love and favour. Grace is full of pleasure, delight, loving-kindness, and goodwill. It is dispensed without regard to the worth or merit of the one who receives it. Therefore, grace is always associated with mercy, love, compassion, and patience. This is the opposite to law, and is the filter through which we can understand how we can live with words like headship and submission and not be dominating or dominated, but in a partnership of equals.

If, as a husband, I am to exercise my role in the way Paul sets out, then my primary consideration is the welfare, comfort, and security of my wife. I cannot do this while dominating, dictating, and insisting that my wife obeys me in everything I desire. This does not fit the model set out, but rather violates the ethical value behind the teaching. If I am going to fulfil my role as a husband then I give up any idea of purely selfish-motivated dominance for the sake of my partnership with my wife. In practice, this means my attitude is that I want to listen to what she thinks and how she feels in any situation or circumstance.

Having this attitude means that we will normally find a mutual togetherness in all we do. If my wife has in her heart the security of feeling that she can trust my love for her, that I will do nothing without giving myself to the welfare of her and our children, then she can freely choose to submit to my love for her. If then, for any reason, we cannot come to a mutually agreeable decision, she can or will trust me to make the right decision based on what we both feel rather than just my personal preferences because she knows I willingly give myself up for the good of our relationship. In my marriage to Mary, if we come to such an impasse that we cannot make a decision together, Mary will say, "Well you have all the information, what are we going to do?" What is more, she wants me to make a decision, she wants me to get on with it and is willing to accept what I may decide. In reality, Mary and I rarely proceed unless we are mutually agreed on the way forward. We are a partnership, but in the rare event that we cannot agree, she is willing and able to trust my heart for her.

The first emphasis is very much on the husband. If he practices this 'giving himself up' then everything else will fall into place. In the ideal marriage, a wife can rely on and trust that her husband's judgement will unreservedly take her opinions into account. She knows that she can, as part of an equal partnership, put her opinion across with conviction in the certainty that she will be listened to. This releases her to be strong in character and full of life and authority while also joyfully submitting to her husband.

This confidence and strong self-esteem can be undermined for either sex, however. If the wife does not trust or respect her husband, she will seek to take control, and if the husband does not trust his wife, the circle of unity breaks down and he begins to dominate. When this happens, it causes them both to withdraw emotionally and become uncooperative because they no longer feel needed or accepted. A husband giving himself up for his wife will never work effectively unless his wife respects him; respect balances the equation and allows real unity as each partner fulfils their destiny. Living this way is an expression of true equality; even though we still have the words, 'head' and 'submit' in our vocabulary, in the context of grace, with each party being allowed to fulfil their roles as male and female, neither husband nor wife will dominate or act without consultation and, where possible, mutual consent. But the question still remains: *Why has God set this ethical value as he has? Why use the words, 'submit' and 'head' to define the partnership between husband and wife?*

I find two possible reasons. The first is the male's ability to dominate because of his greater physical strength, which gives him the ability to force his will if he so desires. The way men treat their wives is very important to God—we see just how important in the book of Malachi. Israel is flooding the altar with tears because God no longer answers their prayers or accepts their offerings. *Why?* Because they were being unfaithful to, and abusing, their wives. God witnessed this abuse and was not happy with them—he actually describes this as 'doing violence to the one he should protect', and warns them to be on their guard and not break the covenant bond they have with their wives (Malachi 2:13-16). In God's eyes, the headship role is one of servanthood, and the husband is charged with the welfare of the whole family; their wellbeing is the purpose for which he is to use his strength. A man flourishes when he is allowed to do that, and becomes frustrated when he is not permitted to do so, withdrawing into himself.

The second reason is that it fits the differences that are found in the intrinsic nature of males and females. The simple truth is that men and women are different—they think differently, have different instincts, and conduct their lives in different but complementary ways. However, none of these differences equate to inequality or imply one gender is inferior to the other.

When Tom commented that he was the team leader in his new Sunday School teaching partnership with Betty because he was a man, he was stating his underlying belief that men are superior to women. This is manifestly untrue, as is evidenced by the capabilities and skills that are on display for all to see in today's world. Women govern countries and are leaders in industry, scientists, firefighters, police officers, soldiers, and anything else you can name. I had to let Tom know that he was not the boss, he was an equal partner in the task of teaching our Sunday School children the ways of God.

∼

For generations, Christians have debated the position of women in marriage, focussing on words like 'submit' and 'obey', while largely ignoring Paul's injunction regarding men, which was revolutionary at the time, trumping Roman law and pointing the way to how godly men were to act. It is in honouring *both* aspects of Paul's teachings that we will rediscover the equal partnership God intended for us while also being freed to celebrate the facets of our personalities and genders that make us unique. And in this redeemed order, not only will our marriages and families flourish, but so, too, will our communities.

God's Word tells us to live in peace with each other. This is so we can reflect the truth that God is a God of peace, not disorder. When we live in a state of disorder, we experience instability, commotion and confusion, whereas when we live at peace with God and one another, we enjoy security and safety. The basic foundation of society is family, and if our marriages and our children are in confusion and disorder, the whole of society is affected.

Mary and I have seen what can happen in a street where one family is out of order and disruptive. When neighbours are disturbed and intimidated, or children are bullied, the whole street can take on a feeling of unease. I recall a single mum who lived in a block of flats in London. She was a believer, and lived on the same floor as a family who were extremely disruptive and abusive to everyone they came across. It all stemmed from the mum and dad who seemed to have no regard for others, and their children, now adults, followed their attitude. This family was in almost complete disorder, and it affected the whole apartment block. Interestingly, this Christian lady, with great grace toward them, began to pray that God would bless this family. Part of the reason they were so disruptive was that the whole family was out of work, which meant they were home all day, every day. This can be a strain on any relationship. As she prayed for them, one by one they began to get jobs, and as they gained jobs the disruption stopped.

The reality is, that marriages established on godly foundations are essential, not only for the wellbeing of the marriage itself and the children that are added, but to all of society.

3

Understanding One Another

Growing up in boys' boarding schools that were staffed almost entirely by men, and only seeing my stepmother sporadically and my sister even less, I entered adulthood with no understanding of women. I thought they were just like men, only built differently. In all honesty, I didn't give any potential distinctions much thought until I married Mary—it was of no consequence in my male-dominated life. Then suddenly, our differences became of the utmost importance!

I could not for the life of me figure out why she wasn't motivated by the same things that I was; why she didn't feel or think the same way I did. The line from the musical 'My Fair Lady' summed up my feelings on the matter: *Why can't a woman be more like a man?* Mary was a mystery to me, and with no mother-figure in my life to look to for advice on how to better understand her, I found myself constantly clashing with this woman I loved. Our situation was also not helped by the fact that the church we were members of had no marriage preparation programme. Quite simply, we both lacked the skills to navigate our differences.

We were committed to one another and there was no way we were going back on the promises we had made, but there did not seem to be much we could do about the situation we found ourselves in. We thought we were just not compatible—perhaps we'd even made a mistake in marrying. Yet with two children, we instinctively knew that it was important to do the best we could for them as well as for ourselves.

We continued in much of a holding pattern for some years until we came upon some books which caused us to realise that men and women are not clones of each other; we have different thought processes, motivations, and needs. This might seem obvious, but for us, it was revolutionary. We were not incompatible, and we had not made a mistake! From this point, on our relationship began to improve. It took a long time to unravel some of the habits that had become ingrained in our relationship, but it was worth it. The more we prayed, read, investigated, talked, and learned from experience—ours and others—the healthier our relationship became. It was not that we never had problems again, but we were much more aware of how to overcome them because we finally understood our differences as male and female.

As I share some of what Mary and I needed to understand about each other, I want to be clear that these are generalisations. Not everything will be true for every man or every woman, because our personalities and upbringings also come into the mix. However, this does not negate the reality that there *are* gender differences. It is only together as male and female that we fully display the image of God, so it only makes sense that each of the sexes reflects different aspects of his being. Our prayer is that as you understand on a very practical level the way God has designed and wired each of you that you would be able to appreciate and honour those differences so that instead of being a source of division, they can draw you into deeper oneness in your marriage.

WHAT A MAN NEEDS TO UNDERSTAND

One of the things I've discovered over the course of fifty-six years of marriage and the countless number of couples we've counselled, is that women are motivated by how they are treated and appreciated. To use modern vernacular, *What is it that turns a woman on?* Like the male, a woman may initially be attracted to a man who is handsome or possesses a particular physique, but appearance is not a long-term driver for her.

Women need more than physical chemistry for their sense of wellbeing in a relationship. In order to thrive, they need to feel appreciated, loved, and cherished—only then will they be able to participate wholeheartedly in the marriage.

The question all husbands must ask is: *How can I express to my wife, day-to-day, how I feel about her?*

Words are one way—especially if one of your wife's love languages is words of affirmation. But saying "I love you" or paying her compliments quickly becomes meaningless if your words are not backed up by action. You must show by your behaviour that you are devoted to her wellbeing. How you do this will require taking into account the way she is uniquely wired, and will no doubt test how well you know your wife! But here are some basic ideas that you can consider:

Be aware of her when you go out together. Pay attention to when she is being shut out of conversations or being left alone while you are busy with your mates. Take the time to introduce her to people you know and she does not, then stay close until you are sure she is settled and accepted—do what you can to make sure she enjoys her time out as much as you do!

Take practical steps to show that you are thinking about her welfare. Open doors for her, allow her to go first, and don't assume that she knows where you are. If you are going to be late, let her know where you are, and if possible, when you expect to be home.

Find things you can do which say, "I love you and I care about you." Some of these may be romantic gestures. You could leave notes or buy flowers or chocolates just for her—whatever you know she loves. But some of them may be more practical. For instance, I noticed that when Mary does the laundry, she first unbuttons all my shirts. I thought, "I can do that when I take a shirt off!" and have done it ever since. Mary had not complained about it, but it blessed her that I would notice and do it for her. *What do you do that makes extra work for your wife?* Do you leave clothes lying around or on the floor for her to pick up? Are there dirty dishes on the kitchen bench or table? Start to pay attention and see how you can help to ease her load.

None of these things should be done in a patronising way, but with genuine love and care. It will all be pointless if you do these things while out or in company but in private do the opposite. Take the time to find out what blesses your wife (ask her if you need to) and show her you love her by what you do, not just by what you say.

Another thing I've learned from experience is that wives need their husbands to *listen in a way that demonstrates they are seeking to understand them*. When she is expressing a viewpoint, she does not need you to interrupt or try to fix things; she wants you to hear her heart and comprehend her struggle. Mary often said to me, "You don't listen!" to which I would reply, "I heard every word," before repeating back to her what she has just said. I was right, I could repeat every word, but I had completely missed the point. There were some fundamental things I had been unaware of.

Firstly, I was not giving my full attention to Mary and what she was saying. I was often distracted by other things around me—I would glance out the window, look at my tablet or book, or worse still, look at my watch. My actions gave her the impression that my mind was elsewhere and that I wished she would just hurry up and finish.

The second problem was that I was always interjecting with suggestions, comments or solutions, often anticipating what I thought she would say. Sometimes I'd even complete her sentence for her. I thought that because it did not bother me when occasionally Mary did this to me, that it should not bother her when I did it to her. But trust me, when a woman is expressing her viewpoint, she does not need you to interrupt her; she needs you to let her finish what she is saying. She wants to feel like you have heard her heart, that you comprehend her struggle and respect her viewpoint.

One of the big differences between men and women is that it brings a sense of wellbeing to a woman if she can share her thoughts and the events of the day without distraction, interjection, or somebody always trying to fix things if there is a problem. Watch how a group of women talk when they are together. They pay attention to one another, sympathising and empathising with what is being said through their facial expressions, the noises that they make, and the occasional emphatic "Yes!" or "Noooo!" Your wife needs the same active listening from you.

I still remember when our children were young and Mary would go out for the evening. She would come home, and as I was often already in bed, she would join me there, turn the light out, and then talk out the evening's events and people. All that was required of me was an occasional grunt to show I was still awake. Once she had reflected on the evening with me, she was able to sleep. But woe betide me if I fell asleep! It wasn't that she resented the fact I had fallen asleep *per se*. It was that if she could not unload her thoughts onto me, everything would just go round and round in her head. I was not listening for my benefit, but for hers.

If you want your wife to be at peace and to feel valued by you, then you need to learn to pay attention when she is sharing her thoughts and feelings. When there is a problem, do not assume she wants you to fix it. Instead, wait until she has finished talking and then ask, "Do you want me to do anything about that?" Most of the time the answer will be no, but occasionally it will be yes. If listening becomes in any way patronising on your behalf, then you need to gain understanding—and quickly. This is loving somebody and being genuinely interested enough to listen and empathise without trying to fix everything.

The final big lesson I've learned, is that wives both need and want their husbands to take responsibility where appropriate. This came as a surprise to both Mary and myself when talking to couples about praying together—almost without exception, wives expressed that they wanted their husbands to take the responsibility to lead them and the family in their spiritual life. Sadly, many wives found themselves having to lead spiritually because their husbands simply would not do it, but that did not mean it was their preference.

However, it goes much further than spirituality. A wife wants to feel her husband has a sense of responsibility for her and their children. It comes back to the instruction Paul gave to husbands in Ephesians 5:25

to 'give themselves up'. This 'giving yourself up' can be described as taking on the responsibility for the family. Taking responsibility is about actively thinking about what is morally right, looking ahead to understand the consequences of any action or inaction for our families, and then making our decisions accordingly. This is not about acting unilaterally; it is about working in partnership with our wives alongside us. They don't want to feel like the buck stops with them alone, but that they are in a relationship with someone who can be relied upon and who is willing to take the strain for them. When you refuse to step up and take responsibility, she feels like she must, and this erodes her respect for you.

One of the most practical ways you can take responsibility and demonstrate your care and love for your wife is to take the lead in arranging regular 'date nights'. This is not to say you organise it all without any consultation, but that you initiate the time together. Make sure it's in the diary, and offer suggestions for what you could do. Being proactive in this communicates to her that you are right alongside her in building your marriage.

As husbands, we are to be like a solid rock, immovable in our passion for the welfare and protection of our families.

WHAT A WOMAN NEEDS TO UNDERSTAND

In the early stages of most boy's lives, girls are almost a non-identity, no more than a bit of a nuisance. This is not true for all, of course. Some do enjoy friendship with girls, but it is a non-sexual thing—mention anything like kissing and you will usually get a disgusted, "yuck!" But then the testosterone kicks in, and a change takes place that is so profound that it completely changes the way a young man looks at a girl. He begins to like what he sees and finds himself attracted to the shape and form of a girl's body, becoming increasingly aware of how his body reacts when he is around the opposite sex. Just like the cartoonists depict, his jaw drops open, the eyes pop out on stalks, and he is left speechless. A lifelong love of the female form has begun; it draws us in, captivating and motivating us. This attraction is never to be used as an excuse for the objectification of women, but it is something that women must understand about their husbands—they respond to what they see.

A man can have a serious argument with his wife, then at bedtime watch her undress and all is forgotten. He wants her, regardless of their disagreement. Unfortunately for him, his wife is completely put off by the row, and the sight of him undressing has no effect on her whatsoever. I remember talking to a couple who were having problems because the wife thought (in her words): *my husband is a sex maniac*. It turned out that this was not the case; she simply did not understand the effect a particular habit of hers had on him. Every evening when she came home from work, she would strip down to her dainty bra and panties, and then wander around the house. This drove her husband mad with desire because he was visually stimulated by seeing her wandering around half-naked; he could not keep his eyes or his hands off her. She, however, did not want to engage in sex at that time, and it was becoming a source of conflict for them. All she needed to do was put on a robe and their problem was solved.

In view of their visual wiring, it also follows that men like their wives to look good. I am not suggesting that we return to the days when women used to dress up for when their men came in from work, but it is worth from time to time, perhaps on your date nights, making a special effort with your appearance to help keep the spark in your relationship.

Another important aspect to understand about the male nature, is that he flourishes when he believes he is valued and needed. Men are both fixers and protectors. If there is a problem, a man likes to fix it; if something is broken, he likes to mend it; if a loved one is threatened (perceived or otherwise), a man likes to protect; if provision is needed, a man likes to be able to provide. This 'fixer' mentality is deeply ingrained.

The problem is that often those he loves do not want him to fix everything—or sometimes, anything. When a man is continually denied the opportunity to help in these ways, his inner 'fixer mentality' closes down and he becomes passive. He believes he is not needed, so he gives up and goes with the flow. In view of this, it is important that you understand that part of being a fulfilled male is knowing that he is needed. It is not that he has to fix everything or has to be at the forefront of every situation, but he does need to know he is not surplus to requirements and that he has a part to play in family life. In other words, his fixer nature needs to be acknowledged even if it is not always required. A simple, "Tell me how I can do this," or "Don't worry, I will call you in if I cannot handle this situation," or even a question like, "Do you think this will work?" will let him know he is wanted for backup should it be needed, and that you value his input.

Connected to this need to make a valuable contribution is that overcorrecting a man's work when he has been trying to help, can result in an undermining of his sense of manhood. When a man can never get anything right, he thinks, *Why bother trying?* because no matter what he does, he can never succeed. Take for instance when a husband washes up and wipes down the bench, only for his wife to come along and wipe the bench all over again. It sends the message, "You did not do it right. This is how you should do it in future, but this time you failed." Or, when a man vacuums the floor, only for his wife to ask, "Did you get right into that corner, and under that chair?" Her questioning sends the message, "You missed a bit. I cannot trust you to do it right. I have to check up on you every time—please get it right if you are going to help, or it is no help at all."

Men like to think they can do anything, and as a general rule, hate asking for help (asking for directions is a classic example!). So when they are constantly corrected, or feel their help is not good enough or is simply not needed, it causes them to withdraw and go into their 'man cave'. A man cave is a place where they may engage in practical tasks, fixing, building, creating or pursuing a hobby, or it may be a place for them to go and contemplate the things they could fix if only they could be left alone and uninterrupted for a while with nobody telling them that there is a better way to do the fixing. The man cave can be a literal place like a shed or a room which is their domain, or it can be a place they withdraw to in their minds. However, wives often follow men into their man caves, trying to get them to come out and talk things through, pointing out that they are being silly and how they were wrong. This is not the right approach. Men need time to process and prepare themselves to relate to their loved one again.

What, then, can women do to help men avoid the need to retreat? You're going to need to be prepared to have some things done differently to how you would do them. Let it go, and stop correcting everything he does. *Does it really matter? Isn't his wellbeing more important than the task at hand?* When you step back and empower a man to do what you've asked without questioning, criticising, or correcting, you live out Paul's command to respect your husband (Ephesians 5:33). That respect will, in turn, enable him to keep desiring to give himself up for you and will help him become the man God intended him to be.

This is true for both of you. As you learn to show respect for and celebrate your differences, be they in gender, personality or gifting, you enable a true partnership and help each other to give expression to the person God created you to be.

PART TWO

Before you Embark on Marriage

4

Choose Wisely

Chris Brown is one of my greatest friends. We worked together for many years as joint church leaders in Bermondsey, Central London. However, unbeknown to me, during this time, our different ways of processing information and reaching decisions caused real issues for Chris. I was an instant processor, with instant opinions and instant solutions for everything, whereas Chris was a reflective thinker who needed time to process before he came to conclusions or decisions—time that I did not give him because of how I was wired. This became increasingly frustrating for him. Now, neither of our approaches was right or wrong, the problem was simply that I did not fully understand his thought processes. We have, I am glad to say, remained good friends in spite of these differences.

If we translate that scenario into a marriage, however, we can see how the potential clash of personalities can be amplified. For many years, my instant opinions caused Mary much frustration because I constantly interrupted her when I thought I knew what she was going to say, or when I thought I had the answer (even if she did not want one!).

If we set our minds to understand each other, we can to some extent see both the possible advantages and the dangers of our individual traits. When you blend two things, you quickly learn about their compatibility. Just try mixing oil and water and you will immediately see that they will not meld together no matter how hard you try. Other substances, however, not only blend well, but also produce something very useful as a result of their union. Take for example, sodium and chlorine, which combine to form salt.

If we are to join our lives to another, we need to know that we can blend and remain compatible. That is not to say that we must be the same. The old saying, 'opposites attract', is true for good reason; two people can be very different and yet still find themselves well-suited for one another. There are, however, some mixtures where the risk has to be known, because if left unattended it has the potential to become very volatile.

When we marry, we have great hopes of living a fulfilled, happy life with our spouse. We envision a partnership that will give us love, support, companionship and security for the rest of our lives. But often our experience falls short of these expectations for the simple reason that, in marriage, we are not only bringing together two different genders, we are also combining different personalities, different ways of processing information and of interacting with the world. Some are introverts, while others are extroverts; some are practical, while others artistic or scholarly; some are active thinkers and respond instantly with solutions, while others need time to reflect before they can reach a decision, and so on. If we want to build a godly and lasting marriage, it is wise to consider how these dynamics interact with one another and to pay attention to the signs—both positive and negative—as to whether this will be a compatible union. Nobody is perfect, but personality differences and faults can seriously affect relationships, and for this reason, you need to carefully consider whether you can live with somebody for the rest of your life. It behoves us to choose our life partner well, with prayer and considerable thought, and not take our future too lightly.

For many of us, falling in love is an emotional experience, and rightly so. However, emotion can mask reality and make it difficult to be objective, blinding us to the very character traits that can eventually push our initial attraction aside. This is why we sometimes need a little help in understanding the good and bad characteristics of our future partner.

Family and close friends are often able to see what you may be blind to, and although it can be difficult to hear somebody else's thoughts about the love of your life, I encourage you to reach out to people in your inner circle that you consider trustworthy and ask what strengths and weaknesses they see in them. Listen, and consider what they have to say—it could just save you a lot of grief. Ultimately, you do not have to agree, but to not consider their counsel is to potentially miss a big clue as to what the future holds.

When I preach and people come and tell me it was wonderful, (it does happen occasionally), I am encouraged. But if somebody comes and tells me that it was very disjointed and not easy to follow (as Mary has on occasions), that is much more difficult to receive. However, which is more beneficial to me in the long-run? I like, and at times need, the praise, but always find that I learn more from the critique, even if, after consideration, I disagree with it. The process of weighing their feedback causes me to assess how I can improve what I am doing and causes me to grow.

But sometimes, not only do we not want to hear concerns about our relationship, we don't want to see them. We have our dreams, and in our minds our partner is a necessary part of those dreams coming true. We're afraid of being alone and are driven by our desire to belong, so we choose to continue in wilful blindness of one another's faults and their long-term implications. Even if we see potential issues, we either think that we can handle anything and believe we can change our future partner, or that it is just not that serious and will all come right after we are married. However, nothing could be further from the truth. Character strengths and weaknesses will only become more magnified once you are living together. Before that, you get to walk away and have your own space, but once you live in the same house, you cannot do that. Your spouse's attributes will only become more obvious to you—and in the case of weaknesses, more troublesome and difficult to handle.

If the 'oneness' that Paul set out in Ephesians is to be lived out—if a wife is to be able to respect her husband, and he to give himself up for her—we cannot ignore the signs that point to potential sources of conflict, or even incompatibility. If you cannot respect someone fully before you get married, then the respect you do have will likely deteriorate over time as it becomes undermined by characteristics you find hard to understand. Likewise, putting someone else's needs first will become increasingly difficult if you realise that you simply do not like some of their personality traits. Prioritising your spouse's wellbeing and care over your own is a big deal, and requires that you love that person very deeply. Do not for one moment think, *I'll just ignore it; I can handle that; it will be alright when we are married.* Ignoring the signs now will simply erode your love and respect for one another down the track, potentially undermining your relationship until it cannot be salvaged. Be willing to be open-minded now rather than with hindsight later.

RECOGNISE THE WARNING SIGNS

Are there signs that predict trouble ahead for you as a couple? I would suggest you take a step back and look objectively at your relationship. It is possible to identify characteristics that reveal what the future may hold. But the time to look for these indicators is during the early days of the developing relationship; it's far more complicated to do so once you are already engaged and planning the wedding. Once the engagement happens, you can feel locked in and unable to exit safely. The same goes for those who move in together—you burn your bridges, as the saying goes, locking yourselves into your relationship, making it much more difficult to reconsider. Once engagement, marriage, or moving in together occurs, many do not have the courage to pull the plug because of the fear of being alone and having to start over.

The signs aren't always big. Often it is very small things that can lead to unhappiness and stress. And sadly, some of those seemingly minor issues lead to very serious problems like domestic violence or emotional abuse. We saw this play out with a couple who we were meeting with for pre-marital counselling. After a few weeks, we found ourselves in a very awkward position as it had become obvious to us that if they married, things were not going to work out well. Their differences in personalities and attitudes indicated that significant conflict lay ahead—not the potential for physical abuse, but for dynamics that would make one or both of them very unhappy. In all our years of pre-marriage counselling we had never sensed so strongly the potential for a negative outcome, and so, with much anxiety, we shared our thoughts with them and asked them to go away and reconsider their decision. They came back to us firm in their decision to get married, and as it was not our mandate to refuse to marry them, we continued with the preparation and they eventually got married.

I wish I was able to report that we were wrong and it all worked out well for this couple, but it did not. The husband was happy but his wife wasn't—in fact, their relationship was a source of much frustration and emotional distress for her. The husband had been slightly disabled through a work accident some years earlier, and was now on a disability allowance. While his injuries were significant enough to prevent him from returning to work, he was not helpless or overly restricted. He could walk, do the housework and gardening, and take himself into town on the bus, enjoying a reasonably active life. His wife worked full-time in the health service, and as a couple, they were reasonably financially secure. On paper, this all sounds like a very good foundation to build a relationship on, *so what was wrong?*

Basically, the husband was neglectful of his wife's needs. For instance, she would come home from a full day's work and he would be eagerly waiting for her. But instead of serving her, he would greet her with, "Hello love, I have put the kettle on. I will have a cup of tea please." This might seem like a very small thing, but imagine coming home from work to this greeting day after day, week after week, and year after year. After the cup of tea, he would tell her that he had put the laundry by the washing machine to make it easier for her. Despite the fact that he was perfectly capable of taking care of such tasks (and had done so prior to their marriage), he expected her to do the housework. During the day, he would go into town and buy things—not things for her, or purchases they had agreed on together, but things for himself that he would then show off to her when she got in from work. The wife was the main breadwinner, while he was at home spending their money without any regard for her. This lack of care for her began to permeate every aspect of their relationship including their sex-life, and in one of our counselling sessions she blurted out her frustration that he showed no consideration for her needs or pleasure when they made love. Over time, all these grievances had built up, creating an unhealthy and unsustainable relationship.

The husband was not a bad man—he just did not get it. He saw nothing wrong with how their relationship functioned and could not understand why these things mattered so much to his wife; the issues she had were such small, inconsequential things in his mind. The problem was that the husband was self-centred, with little to no awareness of the needs of his wife or the effect that his actions had had on her over a period of years. It would have taken such simple steps on his part to put things right, but he lacked the ability to see this, even when we pointed it out to him.

What had sounded the warning bells for us before they got married? We could see that everything revolved around him. His future wife was a gentle, generous, compassionate person who paid attention to his needs and sought to meet them as much as she could, whereas there was little, if any, evidence that he saw her needs and desires, or made any effort to bless or be generous to her. Because of her nature, she could not see the issues even when we raised them with her. The reality is that once married and settled into daily routines, those very issues that at first appeared to be molehills, gradually become mountains. Looking at this relationship through the lens of Ephesians 5, we see that the husband did not give himself up for his wife, and that almost completely eroded his wife's respect for him.

Love demands that we have equal care for one another. When both spouses serve and care, then both feel valued and secure in each other's love. When care and service are one-sided and one is always expected to comply with the wishes of the other, it progressively undermines the other partner.

There are several signs that can reveal this dominance of one person over another. The first might be that you are told and not asked what you would like, or that it's never about you and always about him or her. This was the case for a friend whose husband would buy everything without reference to her—he even purchased new carpet and furniture for their home on his own and she only found out about it when it arrived. Or take the woman I heard on the radio discussing her marriage breakup. She was saying that when she and her husband travelled, he would never offer her the window seat on a flight, and that this depicted the reality about their relationship. Or the scene in a movie I watched where a couple went to a restaurant and he ordered for her without consideration for her wishes. A scenario that plays out in real life all-too-often. All of these indicate someone who may find it difficult or even be unable to put the needs of another above their own.

In the dating period, it can be tempting to feed that self-centeredness. You want to please, so you just go with the flow. But compliance in one person feeds self-centeredness in another, and the burning question is, *What would happen if you pushed back or said no?* That person's response would reveal a great deal. It could reveal simple thoughtlessness and evoke a reaction of immediate remorse and a desire to change—that would be a good reaction. But it may result in a flash of anger which could indicate a problem that would only become more evident once married. A singular event may not mean much, but if it happens again and again? Anger and irritation can, although not always, lead to violence. There are clear clues that indicate this possibility. *How does your prospective partner treat other people who rub him or her up the wrong way? Is there a loss of temper which becomes physical?* If so, this should prompt caution on your part. Now I know that most couples who are dating would say, "He would never do that to me." But if that is so, why is there so much domestic violence? Most victims of domestic violence would have once said the same. Anger, temper tantrums, and frustration can and do lead to violent reactions—which can be exacerbated when alcohol or drugs are added into the mix. If your partner drinks, you are also wise to pay attention to how this influences their personality and reactions.

As your relationship becomes more serious, if you discover attributes and attitudes that are concerning you, you need to talk together about what you are seeing in each other's character. Questions are a very good way of doing this. Let us imagine for a moment that something happens between you, and one of you throws something in frustration or inadvertently lets out a curse. Later, after they have calmed down, you could ask questions like, *What made you react like that? Do such strong reactions happen often? Is this usual for you when you get frustrated? How easy do you find it to control your emotions? I noticed you had difficulty controlling your emotions—how do you control yourself under pressure?*

Don't be put off. This is important. You could even pose a casual question to parents or siblings. *What was he or she like as a child? How did they handle pressure as a teenager?* In this way you are gently probing, informing yourself of the fault lines in each other's personalities.

These are some of the factors to be mindful of as you consider how a relationship may develop in the long term. It is vital for your wellbeing that they are not ignored but faced up to before it is too late. However, they are not the only signs you need to consider. It's also important to look at what indicates the potential for a successful marriage.

REASONS FOR CONFIDENCE

One of the things that can help us recognise why we have reason to be confident in our relationship is understanding the nature of true love. 1 Corinthians 13:4 teaches us that love is patient and kind. According to one dictionary, patience is 'being able to accept or tolerate delays, problems, or suffering without becoming annoyed or anxious', while kindness considers somebody else's needs and desires. 1 Corinthians also tells us that love does not envy or boast; it is not arrogant or rude. It does not insist on its own way; it is not irritable or resentful (vv.4-5, ESV). If we applied this definition of love to the husband in our earlier story, his kindness would have said, "Come and sit down while I get you a cup of tea, and don't worry about the laundry, I did that this afternoon." If he had been to town that day, he might have presented her with the flowers he had bought her. And his desire to put her first and to not insist on his own way would have meant that he was willing to make the necessary changes when confronted with the issues in their marriage.

Another thing that love does is to bear the burdens of the one that is loved (Galatians 6:2). The wife in our story bore and embraced the burdens of her husband's disability. She was not resentful, but was accepting and willing to endure, which is why she still wanted to marry him. You can give and give when you know the one you love cannot give back, but you become wearied when the one you love is able to give, yet is only prepared to receive.

We all have faults, we all display jealousy, and we all have a tendency to be self-seeking. Yet when we love another deeply, we deliberately place ourselves second and promote the one we love to be first. If we both do this, then the result is an amazing partnership that is a pleasure to be in. Love covers our faults, and this grace towards one another causes our good attributes to come to the fore (1 Peter 4:8). Always remember that when you are living together full-time, character flaws become more obvious, but good character traits bring security to the relationship. While you are dating, make 1 Corinthians your litmus test: *Are the attributes of love present in how you interact with and treat each other?*

As you seek to determine the answer to this question, understand that none of us are perfect. We all have weaknesses and must be willing to learn and grow. Jesus teaches that we should first of all look to our own faults, and that means we have to be open to questions about ourselves (Matthew 7:3-5). The real issue lies in how we respond when our faults are exposed. *Are we willing to acknowledge them and receive help to make the necessary changes?* The attitude of 'take me as I am' is one to run a mile from.

We are God's people, and that means repentance and change are an integral part of our lives. We are all seeking on a journey with God. We want to be more like him, and desire to please him with our lives. When we marry another person, our roads to God are joined. We walk together into his will. But in order to do this, we must be on the same page. This is why I have put a lot of emphasis on each individual considering one another's character—it's important that you know whether you will be able to successfully blend your lives. If you decide to pursue marriage, always seek to help one another in places of weakness and use your strengths for the glory of God. Nevertheless, don't ignore the signs. The positive signs will give you confidence and encourage you, whereas picking up the negative could just save you a lot of grief and stress.

5

The Battle of the Outlaws

One of the major influences in our lives are our parents, grandparents, and wider family culture. We might like to think this is not so, but in reality, we have been living with and absorbing their example from the day we were born, watching how they relate to one another, how they parent and work and generally manage life. Whether good or bad, we often internalise that influence to a larger extent than we consciously appreciate.

When you come together as a couple, you both bring this influence into your marriage. Your family frameworks may be very different, and hold the potential for conflict if not understood. The same can be said for the expectations of both sets of parents. I like to call it *the battle of the outlaws*. This is not in any way to be contentious or disrespectful towards either family, but to emphasise the very real tension that can exist because of these sometimes-opposing examples.

But before we delve deeper into navigating these differences and, at times, conflicting expectations, I want to offer a word of advice. The Bible is very definite when it comes to how we are to relate to our parents—we are to honour them. To honour somebody is to value them, to esteem them highly, or to put in the negative, to not neglect them. It is the only command given in Scripture that carries with it a blessing—that you may live long and prosper in your life (Exodus 20:12).

Pause for a moment and think about your parents. They are, in the vast majority of cases, the ones who have unreservedly loved you more than anybody else in your life so far. From the day you were born they have cared for you and taught you, giving you guidance and assistance. Certainly, they will have not got everything right nor always said the right thing, and you may well have clashed with them at times—particularly during your teenage years—but they have been there for you and with you every step of the way. So, as you get married, give consideration to how you can honour them as a couple, not only on the day of your wedding, but in your ongoing relationship with them and with your in-laws.

HONOURING YOUR PARENTS

Figuring out how to incorporate both sets of parents into your relationship is an aspect of marriage which can cause tension for many couples. One mum, who only had sons, remarked that daughters are more likely to be strongly orientated toward their parents than sons are. She added that because men generally follow their wives' lead, this can result in the couple spending more time with the wife's family than the husband's, as had been the case with one of her sons. This imbalance had been particularly hard for her when it came to how they spent their time over Christmas and other holidays, but her son was extremely protective of his wife's feelings, and she found that she was unable to say anything because of the possibility it would upset her daughter-in-law.

    This is not the only family I've known to have this experience. In truth, there is a natural tendency, as I have observed over time, for women to have a maternal link to their mothers, a strong bond which stands firm regardless of how long ago they left home. Men, on the other hand, while still loving their parents, do not typically have that same emotional bond or need. This is, of course, a generalisation, as for some this is reversed, especially when parents are dysfunctional and childhood has been very difficult, or when parents have died, and they find in their in-laws real acceptance and love.

Regardless of where the bond lies, you can create a culture in your marriage that honours one another's parents. You can determine in your hearts and in the rhythms of your life that you will not neglect either set of parents or favour one over the other. As I discovered, this will likely take some forward planning and thinking on your part.

My parents once complained that they had not seen much of me, and on reflection, I realised that they were right. My diary was full and consequently, they had been squeezed out—not through lack of desire but through busyness on my part. I had been inadvertently neglecting them and needed to find a way of including them in our lives. The solution I came up with was that at the start of each year, I would put an appointment in my diary to see them every six weeks. I then sent them the dates. At first they were offended by receiving a year's worth of 'appointments', but I explained that I wanted to make them a priority and that by them knowing the dates, I had already decided I would have to reschedule anything else that came up. They got the point and appreciated my efforts to honour them with my time.

Sometimes the expectations of our extended families go far beyond how much time we should spend with them, and begin to encroach onto how the marriage itself should be conducted. This is why it is vital that we not only understand our family dynamics, but also take the time to determine what we want our own marriages and families to look like.

ESTABLISHING YOUR OWN IDENTITY

Once, while on a ministry trip to India, my colleagues and I were invited to a wedding. For the initial ceremony, the bride was dressed in western-style bridal fashion with a white dress and veil. For the reception, however, she and her new husband changed into traditional Indian dress and were seated on two throne-like chairs which were elevated higher than their guests so that they could be admired. The food was classic Indian wedding food—very rich and, of course, all very spiced.

Yet behind this lavish setting lay a serious clash of cultures—not between western and Indian as you might expect, but between Christian practice versus the local traditions.

The newly-married couple were devoted to Christ and fully involved in their local church, but the parents of the bride and groom were not believers and expected this new couple to conform to their traditions. In their community it was customary for the new bride to leave her home after the wedding and move in with her in-laws, where she would be trained to look after her husband in the manner he was used to. The daughter-in-law was often considered a sort of 'free domestic servant' under her mother-in-law's control and at her bidding.

However, this is not the biblical pattern. In Ephesians, when Paul writes about the relationship between husband and wife, he ends with this quote from Genesis 2:24: "For this reason a man will leave his father and mother and be united to his wife, and the two will become one flesh" (Ephesians 5:31, NIV). This principle of 'leaving and cleaving' was also articulated by Jesus himself in Matthew 19:5. It is backed up in three authoritative ways within Scripture: in Creation, by Jesus, and later by Paul.

Knowing this young couple were facing considerable demands to submit to the traditions of their parents and their culture, the pastor who married them chose this passage in Ephesians as the text for his message during the ceremony. He spoke very strongly on the subject, and at the time, I remember thinking, *Boy, he is laying this on thick!* He later told me that he felt compelled to speak as firmly as he did because of the intense pressure being put on the couple by the groom's parents. He was not speaking to the bride and groom—they were already convinced—but to the parents.

What this scriptural principle teaches us, is that when a marriage partnership is formed, the couple are to set up a new home and forge their own identity as a family unit. Jesus makes it clear that they are no longer two but one (Matthew 19:6). And while they are each connected to their existing families, a new 'branch' has sprouted. This independence is not what many of us have perceived it to be in western culture—it is not encouraging us to separate and pursue an individualistic lifestyle. We are still a part of the whole; still part of a larger tree. Family is family, and we must learn to honour and maintain both our interconnection *and* our independence as a new partnership.

But it can be a struggle to allow this new branch to grow and form, even if you have been brought up with a good model of what marriage and family life looks like. Whether you entered marriage with a good example or a bad one, Christian or non-Christian, it remains the framework that has been built into you and that you subconsciously expect to carry into your own married life. Because you both carry these inner expectations, your presumptions may be very different.

Buried within your parental examples is a code of conduct. When these two different codes come together, there is the potential for them to clash—perhaps in ways you did not see coming. You may have taken for granted that the way your family operated was the norm, so much so that you may not have thought about it or analysed it. It just is, and consequently, we often don't foresee the need to discuss these 'codes' in advance.

Take for example the cooking of meals. Let's say that in the bridegroom's household, the women do all the cooking and meal preparation. The men might be given the largest helpings and offered seconds first, and what is more, the men never do the washing up. It is normal for men of such a household to accept this favourable division of responsibility, sometimes without question, because they've never known any other arrangement; it is completely normal to them.

Now let's consider the bride's experience. Let's say her upbringing has been very different—none of these gender stereotypes or attitudes were present. Everybody was treated equally, with Dad often doing the cooking while everyone else mucked in with clearing and washing up. This sharing of household tasks between all family members was normal for her.

With these wildly disparate experiences and inbuilt codes, can you imagine the clash of cultures that awaits this new household?! Add into the mix differences of personality and gender and it could be a time-bomb waiting to explode. If we want to reduce the risk of our parental examples dividing us and instead form a healthy new family branch, we need to become aware of what we do and do not want to bring into our union. This is part of the dating and marriage preparation process.

Over the years, Mary and I have developed three practices to help couples understand where they are coming from, and to reach a decision together about how they want things to work in their marriage. As you read through these steps, it is essential that you consider the way forward through the eyes of your future partner, not just your own. The goal is to come to a mutual position, taking the best from both families and from other marriages you may know and admire. Remember that these ideas and plans will evolve over time—they should never be set in stone.

The first thing you must do is *observe*. When we observe, we slow down to really look at something. But it is *how* we look that determines what we see. The Bible tells us that it is possible to 'see and yet not truly see', or to 'hear and yet not actually hear,' or by implication, understand (Jeremiah 5:21). If we are going to be able to see and hear with understanding, we need wisdom.

One of the attributes of wisdom is the ability to discern the outcome of a particular path. By looking at where your choices and habits will lead you, you will be able to see any changes that need to be made. As you thoughtfully consider the background that your future partner has come from, and observe his or her family life, you will begin to understand the culture that has shaped them. As you compare their family's culture with your own, you will begin to sense the values that are important to you and that you want to develop within your new family life. If you are both doing this, you will quite naturally form a shared desire about how you want your life together to look. This for some can be quite different from their parental example, but it is usually a mixture of both.

Once you have made your observations, you need to take the time to *discuss* what you have learned. This is not a formal, "Let's sit down and discuss the nature of our shared culture" type of thing, but more of an ongoing conversation as you go about your day-to-day life. You need to be aware, as you approach these discussions, of the danger of seeing things only from your perspective, and of being judgemental and dismissive of everything in the 'out-laws' culture. This danger is exactly why we use the term 'out-laws' rather than 'in-laws'. Everything in your partner's family lifestyle is 'outlawed'! I am exaggerating to make a point, of course, but I want to be very clear: *You must be willing to consider one another's viewpoint and to change.* You need to take the best and not ridicule the rest!

The final thing you need to do is to *ask questions.* Questions are a good way of clarifying and understanding what you see and hear. They help you to explore the kind of family life you want to cultivate together. Going back to our example of the men being given preferential treatment at dinner time, you could ask, "Why are the men in your family always offered seconds first?"

This in itself opens up many other questions, such as, *As a woman, how does that make you feel? Do you know where that habit came from? I wonder why your mum allows that continue? Do you think it's mostly your mum or your dad who sets the tone in the family?* As you seek to understand your future partner's family culture, avoid making condemning statements. The desired outcome of conversation is to bring you together and help you develop your approach as a couple, not to put up barriers or drive your partner into a defensive corner.

Rather than expecting one spouse to adopt the culture of the other, intentionally define and create your own. One-sided domination shows no empathy or consideration for others, and is a great danger to the long-term health of a marriage. When one partner insists that things are always done a certain way or to a particular standard, it creates emotional pressure that, over time, reduces a person's confidence, particularly in the one being dominated. The problem is that people are often unaware that it is happening, which is why it is the responsibility of each partner to be observing, initiating discussion, and asking questions, always out of concern for the welfare of their partner rather than themselves. If you do this, you will reap the rewards of peace, confidence, and unity within marriage.

As you forge your own marital identity, there will undoubtedly be times where your extended family seek to influence how you develop your home-life as a couple. Sometimes this will need to be addressed directly, and in such instances, it is not the in-law, but the son or daughter, who needs to talk with their relatives and put a stop to any pressure to conform to their expectations and habits. Know how you want to conduct your married life and stick to it regardless of the hints and suggestions coming from those outside of your relationship. But at the same time, stay open as a couple to the ways your marriage can develop and evolve over time in order to stay healthy. Be aware of how your behaviours impact your partner, and don't be afraid to explore new ideas and ways of doing things that allow your 'branch' to grow into maturity.

6

Daily Life

There was a time when our daughter and her family were living with Mary and me when Mary became quite ill. I needed to do the laundry but I had one big problem: I did not know how to operate the washing machine. My big mistake was confessing this to everyone. I went into the lounge-room where they all were, and asked, "How does the washing machine work?" My granddaughter was incredulous and also somewhat disgusted that I did not know how to do the laundry—and I understood why! Household chores tend to be shared between both husband and wife much more now than in previous generations. This is especially true when both partners are working, or as in our case, are retired and at home together. One *would* expect that we would both be involved in all the chores a household requires. But don't be too quick to judge, because while we want to avoid assigning tasks according to stereotypical gender roles, the reality is that within every marriage partnership there are preferences and differences that need to be negotiated as you determine how your home will practically function.

So why did I not know how to do the laundry? Because Mary loves housework, even ironing—crazy, but true! Mary enjoys all aspects of keeping the house clean and tidy and does not want my help. I offer and have told her that if she wants me to do anything she only has to ask and I'll be there, but she seldom takes me up on it. On the other hand, Mary does not like gardening, so anything outside—including cleaning windows—is my contribution to our life together. The one thing Mary does enjoy doing in the garden is to harvest the vegetables. So, I plant the garden and maintain it, and she enjoys collecting its fruits. Similarly, when one of us cooks, the other washes up. For us, these arrangements work. We are both in agreement and very content with the way we do things, and feel no pressure to change or conform to how anyone else thinks we should be managing our household chores. There's a rhythm to how we do things but we're not locked into how we've arranged our day-to-day chores. If I need to help Mary, or she needs to help me, then there is no hesitation in doing so.

Every married couple needs to come to a mutual arrangement in regard to the sharing of domestic chores. We can work to develop the principles that underpin our marriage, get all of our ducks in a neat row and have all the theory worked out, but we still have to live in ease and find harmony and peace in our day-to-day lives together. And for that, we need to determine our *how*.

ACKNOWLEDGE YOUR INBUILT EXPECTATIONS

In the past, chores and household responsibilities were often assigned based on what was considered 'women's work' and 'men's work'. Women looked after the home and children, while men went to work to provide the family income. This was certainly true in our home: When our first child was born, Mary stayed at home to look after him and I continued to work to provide for us. It naturally followed that Mary looked after the housekeeping and did most of the cooking, while I did the heavy chores, decorating, and mending.

But things have changed dramatically in just a few generations, and generally speaking, both partners now continue to work even when they have children. The stereotype of men who go to work and women who stay at home has gone—which means that the way we view our roles inside the home has to change as well. With the responsibility for providing an income much more shared today than it was for our forebears, we must also share the day-to-day chores that are necessary for running a household so the burden doesn't fall unfairly on one spouse. How you do that is a personal choice, one which nobody else can decide for you. You have to work it out for yourselves, just as Mary and I have done.

As you figure these things out, be aware of the example your parents set and how it shapes your expectations—particularly if they have had a very stereotypical way of approaching chores. What may have worked very well for your parents may not necessarily work for you. Some men who were brought up in an atmosphere with clearly-defined traditional roles may find it particularly difficult to embrace a new way of doing things. But it's important that if that has been your experience you don't simply expect your wife to conform to how your parents did things. If you do, the result will likely be tension, irritation, and resentment—especially if she is working full-time and you are still expecting her to do most of the chores.

Whether based on tradition, gender stereotypes, or your familial example, as we explore the more practical side of living together, I encourage you to identify and intentionally put aside your inbuilt expectations and to develop your own household patterns based on your unique needs and availabilities as a couple.

FIND YOUR OWN PATTERN

We all have strengths and weaknesses, things we are good at, things we like doing, and things we don't like doing but sometimes have to! For example, I don't particularly enjoy washing up after a meal, whereas Mary doesn't mind it—but that does not mean that on the nights she cooks she should also have to wash up. While our preferences will sometimes fall into a convenient pattern, as they have tended to for Mary and me, the division of labour cannot always be based on this. We all have to do some of the things we don't like in order to keep the household running smoothly and fairly (and if neither of you like doing a particular task I highly recommend you do it together!). "You like doing that and I like doing this" is quite simply not always practical, which is why you need to be flexible, adapting your approach as circumstances change.

At first, you will almost certainly share all the chores equally, especially if you are both working full-time. But as you move through the seasons of parenting and being empty-nesters, and later, retirement, these divisions will need to shift to recognise these changes. I had coffee with a friend who had recently retired but his wife was still working, and he was telling me that he had been able to bless his wife by taking responsibility for the housework, washing and cooking so that when she came home, she was able to relax without worrying about any chores. When she retires, things will change and it will become a shared task again, but for now, he has more capacity to tend to the home. The time that each partner has in any given season will likely be a big factor in your own negotiations about how the household will run, but never take your spouse or their time for granted. Keep talking, and approach things with an open mind, being aware of each other's needs as you decide who does what. Being in agreement is key to your home running smoothly.

In addition to being in agreement about who does what, you also need to communicate your expectations about when and how chores will be done if you want to avoid unnecessary strife. This is best illustrated by friends of mine (let's call them John and Sue), who were both working full-time. They were willing to share chores and had agreed on how they would divide them—Sue would dust and clean the kitchen and John would do the vacuuming—but they were experiencing real conflict over the timing of those chores.

Sue wanted to get the chores done as soon as possible on a Saturday morning so that they were freed up to enjoy the rest of their weekend break. John, on the other hand, loved nothing better than to have a good long lie-in on Saturday mornings. The conflict that surrounded these differences overshadowed and often ruined their weekends. Sue felt that she was let down by her husband's laziness and John felt deprived of his cherished

Saturday lie-in. They were both resentful and moody and niggled at each other all day because of the strain this situation put on their relationship.

The solution for Sue was a matter of trust, and for John, it was a matter of promise. John promised Sue that he would take care of the vacuuming when he got up, allowing Sue to happily go about her chores at the time she preferred, confident he would keep his word. She got to enjoy relaxing for the rest of the weekend, and John got to enjoy his lie-in. All the tension they had been experiencing disappeared overnight, and weekends became peaceful occasions.

The lesson we can learn from this couple is that tensions can build up in a marriage when one spouse feels pressure to conform to the other's timing or sense of the way things should be done. You need to keep in mind that you may be different in how you tackle things, and both of you should respect that. You also need to learn to recognise where the responsibility lies.

A friend of mine once had a word with me about her husband. Things had reached a point where she felt as though she could do nothing right—if she pulled the curtains, he would immediately get up and straighten them. If she dusted the mantelpiece, he would rearrange everything. His actions were undermining her confidence, and she felt pressure to do things differently. In reality, his response had nothing to do with her and everything to do with how he was wired, and the problem was easily solved. When I asked her what he did for a living and discovered he was an art director in the film industry, the penny dropped—he was simply doing what he did every day at work, instinctively finessing his surroundings. Once she understood this, she was able to relax knowing it was not that she had 'done it wrong', but that he was just fussy about minute details in a way she was not. From then on, she just let him get on with it.

But these preferences can be disruptive in marriage. Take the young couple who both worked full-time and shared the chores until their first child was born. Then the wife switched to working part time. Because she was home in the afternoons with their child, she would cook dinner and do the laundry, but they still shared chores over the weekends. However, the problem was that their standards were not the same. The wife would leave the lunchtime dishes in the sink and place the laundry in a pile on the sofa to put away later, while the toys her son played with were left on the floor to be put away after he had gone to bed. But her husband hated the washing-up not being done, could not stand laundry on the sofa, and liked a house that was tidy when he came in. And what's more, he did not keep quiet about his views, shouting at his wife and getting upset with her.

The reality of the situation was that there was not a lot of time left in the afternoons, especially with a young child to look after. The husband's expectations were too high and his standards were not shared by his wife. They were not necessarily wrong, just different. This husband needed to understand that, even though she was home for three or four hours a day, it was not enough time to do all he expected of her. He also needed to understand that his wife's way of doing things was different—she was not the perfectionist that he was—and to recognise that the way he was communicating his expectations was creating anxiety about his homecoming at the end of each day.

We suggested that when he arrived home, he ignored what he saw and instead greeted his wife and child warmly, giving them his attention and taking an interest in how their day had been. When he had done that, he could do the washing up and tidy some toys without putting pressure on his wife. *Why?* Because he was responsible for his standards, not her. He did just that, and the tension between them disappeared.

We were able to help this couple because we were considering the problem from outside of their situation. When they looked at it, they only saw their own perspective and standards—they needed to learn to seek the welfare of one another first, putting their own preferences second, and seeing the situation through the other's eyes. This young husband was able to understand that if he wanted to have things his way, he needed to take responsibility for getting it done. His wife then needed to let him do this without feeling she was failing.

Love does not press its own standards onto others, but makes allowances for each other's differences. This grace is not, however, an excuse for laziness. We all have to pull our weight and work together for mutual satisfaction. It is unfortunately the case that sometimes one partner has a tendency for laziness, or, like me, is an expert procrastinator, and the other may be tempted to just get on with it, doing the other person's chores as well as their own, thereby setting a precedent that will be difficult to change once established. There's no one set way to handle such situations, but there are principles for how to manage them in a way that honours God and one another. Don't shout and lose your temper; simply decide whether you are going to take care of what is not being done, or whether you will simply leave it for them. If I have a picture frame to mend and keep putting it off, Mary does not rush in and do it—she quietly asks me when I am going to do it and then leaves it with me. Eventually, I do get it done!

There remains, in the background of all these day-to-day chores and divisions of responsibility, the concept of partnership, a facing of the practicalities of daily life together. If one of you feels resentful, then something is wrong. If one of you feels overwhelmed, something is wrong. Behind such feelings sits a lack of care, observance, and enquiry from one to the other. If we love, we care. If we care, we observe and are watchful of the one we love. *Are they overdoing things? Are they showing signs of strain?* Occasionally we need to take the time to enquire, and ask questions like, "How are things going with you? Are you okay with the way I am getting things done around the house? How do you think we are managing the running of the home?"

Be aware that the rhythms you create will evolve over time; do not expect them to remain static, because as your circumstances change, so too will the way you organise your lives. The way you start will almost certainly not be the way things will remain over time. But so long as you are careful to maintain your concern for one another's wellbeing in whatever you are doing, peace will rest on your home.

PART THREE

Foundations for a Healthy Marriage

7

Intercommunication

A friend arrived at church one Sunday morning without her husband and wasted no time in telling me that he was on the golf course for the club championships. It was clear that she did not approve one little bit with his decision when she rather proudly told me, "I never said a word, Bob, I just let him go and hoped his conscience would speak to him." I must admit to laughing out loud when she said this, because although she might not have uttered a single word, she had undoubtedly made her disapproval known. She may not have used words, but the look would have been enough!

Communication is defined in Webster's dictionary as 'the imparting or interchange of thoughts, opinions, or information by speech, writing, or signs.' This tells us that communication is much more than words. Words are important, for sure, but our tone, facial expressions, gestures, and actions all play a part in what and how we communicate.

From the time we are born, we rely on facial recognition, learning to read the expressions of those around us for signs of love and acceptance, but also for warning signals. Facial expressions can make us feel safe or afraid, loved or unloved. This continues into adulthood—as we listen to words, we also watch a person's face to determine their reliability and true intentions. *Are they speaking for our benefit or their own?* The face communicates much more than we realise, telling us things words cannot.

In addition to facial expressions, we also use gestures and actions to reinforce what we are saying. These actions can be inclusive or exclusive. When we use words like 'you' and 'you're' with our finger extended, we are generally communicating aggressively, whereas when we use words like 'we' and 'us' with the palms of our hands toward ourselves, we communicate inclusivity.

If you are to communicate effectively with your spouse, you are going to need to not only choose your words wisely, you also need to recognise how the messages you send them are impacted by these non-verbal components. How you communicate with one another—your *intercommunication*—is going to be one of the most critical and foundational building blocks in your marriage.

THE GLUE OF YOUR RELATIONSHIP

I have used the word intercommunication rather than communication because it has a sense of interdependence, and it is this interdependence that paves the way for your intimacy, for two becoming one flesh. But while the emphasis of 'one flesh' is often placed on your physical joining together, you cannot become truly one without first having a joining of spirit, heart, and mind. Relationships that are based solely on physical attraction are simply not sustainable; it is these more intrinsic elements of your chemistry that matter most. The heart represents your emotions and the need to experience acceptance and belonging, while the mind is the intellectual or thinking part of who we are, but even if there is an emotional and intellectual attraction, this, too, will eventually be hindered if you are not united in spirit.

One of the problems our world faces is that relationships have been reduced to physical attraction, which almost immediately gets turned into a sexual relationship. The issue is that we then tend to judge the relationship by the quality of the physical experience, which can mask any incompatibility of the spirit, heart, and mind. This is why following the biblical pattern for 'oneness' is so important—and necessary for the longevity of your relationship. When we save our physical joining for after we marry, we are able to spend the time beforehand really getting to know one another—to test our spiritual, emotional, and mental compatibility without sex masking any differences between us. When we are compatible in these ways, it is much easier to establish healthy intercommunication. This underpins how effectively you are able to talk about and build some of the other foundational aspects of your marriage.

You could say that intercommunication is the glue that keeps everything else together, but over our years of marriage counselling, we have found four aspects of the marriage relationship—intercommunication, intimacy, money, and your shared faith as a couple—that are key to the health and success of a marriage. When all four are attended to, they enable you to keep your relationship alive and fresh; neglect them and you open yourselves to the possibility of an increasingly stagnant and unfulfilling union. We often refer to these four areas as 'living foundations', for the simple reason that they must be actively pursued and maintained to be of optimum benefit. However, beware of making them a routine or a law that you must suffer through. Make them yours in a way that suits your personalities; they need to fit your relationship and not be a shadow of somebody else's practices.

We will explore the living foundations of intimacy, money and faith in the coming chapters, but for now, we encourage you to pray for wisdom to truly hear and understand one another as you discuss these sometimes delicate subjects. Remember, this is not about making your point or getting your way, but about coming together as one to build a marriage you can truly enjoy. And therein lies one of the most important lessons about intercommunication: *You must learn to listen to one another.*

THE ART OF LISTENING

We all have an opinion which we would like to air; we want to be understood and intensely dislike being misunderstood. When we feel like what we've said is being misconstrued, we push harder, repeating ourselves again and again until often, we find ourselves in a heated argument. To be frank, this is something I struggle with—I find myself with an answer or an opinion on almost every subject that comes up. And I know I'm not alone in this. I well remember a husband who came to us for help because every discussion he had with his family turned into a conflict. He was frustrated that his family just could not seem to understand his viewpoint. In his mind, his perspective was true and valid, but because he felt so misunderstood, he kept pushing his case to get them to understand, only it was coming across as arrogance.

One of the biggest problems when it comes to communication is when we are seeking only to make a point. But our perspective will often be in opposition to our spouse's, and if our only focus is having our opinion heard, divisive arguments are inevitable. If we want peace and harmony in our marriages, we need a different approach; we must train ourselves to listen before we speak. Our natural tendency to be defensive means it can be hard to make this switch from focusing on having our viewpoint understood to seeking to understand another's, but it is necessary for the health of our relationships.

Believe me, I know firsthand how hard this change is to make. Despite how long we have been married, it's only in recent years that I have become fully aware of the need to listen and not interrupt, and it's hard to change a habit of a lifetime! We have a ninety-year-old friend who comes to the golf club for lunch with us. I have noticed that when someone is speaking and he interrupts, he immediately stops, apologises, and encourages you to carry on with what you are saying. It's a reminder to me that even if I trip up and make the mistake of interrupting, I can still course-correct and return to actively listening to the other person.

The objective of listening is to understand or fully comprehend what somebody is saying. But as we've already established, this isn't as easy as it sounds, because while we are listening, we are usually also forming our own opinion about what is being said which often causes us to interrupt the other to make that opinion known! This is why we must intentionally train ourselves to listen well.

Training requires sustained instruction and practice. But it also requires a mindset of yourself second and your spouse first. You seek their welfare, you care about them and want them to be happy, and so you listen, trying to understand what it is they are saying and feeling in any given situation. Just imagine for a moment what the outcome would be in marriages if both husbands and wives adopted this attitude, showing a deep and genuine interest in what the other was thinking and feeling. The result would be a very peaceful union indeed.

There are two practical ways in which you can set yourselves up to aid your intercommunication. Both of these things need to be made into habits—a settled or regular practice that you adopt and do not readily give up.

The first is that you must plan to spend time together regularly and then make that plan happen! Life is busy, so while you need to be flexible about when and where you meet, you do need to be steadfast in ensuring you regularly and consistently carve out space to focus on your relationship. Use this time to check in with one another and talk about how you are feeling, what you've been thinking about, what you're each dreaming about and wanting in this season, and how you're doing at supporting one another. Depending on how you're wired, these conversations may flow naturally, or you may need to ask probing questions like, *How have you been doing recently? Do you feel as if I listen to you and seek to understand you? Is there any way I have neglected to communicate with you?*

These questions lead us to our second habit: You must train yourself to listen and comprehend what your partner is saying without interruption. Wait until they have finished what they want to say and then check with them that you have understood by repeating back what you have heard. For example, after your partner has finished speaking you might respond by saying, "This seems to be important to you, so to make sure I have got it right, was this what you were saying?" Then repeat back to them what you understood and ask again, "Did I get that correct?" If you haven't, ask for clarification until their response is, "Yes, that's what I meant." Once you are both on the same page, then you can offer your perspective, but remember to always speak with their best interests at heart.

Communication gives us intimate knowledge of our partner's loves, fears, and desires, allowing us to understand them as nobody else does. But it is a two-way process; we both need to learn to share and to listen. In this way, intercommunication involves both 'revealing' and 'receiving'. It is having the confidence to share your inner-self with the one you are joined to; to trust them with your deepest thoughts and feelings. We all need to feel that we have a safe space in which to process and be heard and understood, but this trust can very easily be lost by carelessness on the part of the listener. If the listener is always distracted, looking at their phone or out the window or around the room, or continually checking their watch, these are all indications that the 'receiver' is not listening attentively. On the other hand, eye contact, a nod, or an exclamation where appropriate, all encourage the speaker to continue. When something is being revealed, it needs to be effectively received.

It is the same in our relationship with God. We can get to know God through what he has revealed in his Word, but only if we pay attention and take it in. The prophet Hosea makes this point when he tells Israel that God's people were being destroyed by "lack of knowledge" (Hosea 4:6, NIV). They had rejected the knowledge of God, and that rejection made any ongoing relationship between them and God very difficult. It is the same in our marriages—we can love deeply, but without understanding even the best relationship will become unhealthy. Proverbs 19:2 tells us, "Enthusiasm without knowledge is no good." When communication breaks down and we stop taking the time to truly know each other, then the relationship itself becomes fractured.

To avoid this fate, you must each train yourselves to put the other first. If you both do this, you put yourselves in a win-win position; you will gain life and grow together in your oneness. We can apply the principle of a seed—if a seed never dies, it cannot produce any fruit, but if the seed dies it sprouts into a new life. Jesus said this is an example of people who want to preserve their lives, to look out for their own interests (Matthew 10:39). When we are willing to die to ourselves and put our spouse first, we create an opportunity for something new and beautiful to grow in our marriage. The alternative is that we fight for our position, and in doing so, we devour and destroy one another (Galatians 5:15).

It needs to be stated that how we feel can be misleading, because our feelings do not always match up to the truth. For this reason, we should be careful about using feelings to exclusively judge situations. I have found that the feelings I have do not always match reality. For example, in some situations, I have felt rejected and not valued, but I have then realised that this is not true—I am not rejected, I just feel like I am. Did this make my feelings irrelevant? No, it just means that the people who value me have not been communicating by word or action how valued I am. It is good to *know* I am valued, but it is great to *feel* it as well. In marriage, we can love somebody and value them but if we neglect to communicate that, it can leave the other person feeling they are not properly valued or loved. Such neglect affects everything we do and communicates unhappiness to our partner.

The Bible gives some good principles which we can apply to our intercommunication skills: "Do not judge others, and you will not be judged. Do not condemn others, or it will all come back against you. Forgive others, and you will be forgiven. Give, and you will receive. Your gift will return to you in full—pressed down, shaken together to make room for more, running over, and poured into your lap. The amount you give will determine the amount you get back" (Luke 6:37-38).

The more we listen without judgement but with understanding, the more life will flow back into our marriage. This is something that I have come to understand over time and that I wish I had known when Mary and I were young—it would have saved us a lot of heartache. The reality is that this kind of sacrificial intercommunication does not come easy to most of us; we have to work at it until it becomes an ingrained habit. This means that we need to be patient, knowing that our partner will not always get it right, and of course, that neither will we. But it is worth persevering to create a relationship in which you both feel seen, heard, and valued.

8

Intimacy[1]

Back in the days when most people, including non-Christians, did not live together before getting married, I was asked to film a wedding. I heard later that the groom was rather embarrassed when he found out the cameraman was also a church minister—he'd come out of the church after his ceremony shouting, "Now we can have sex!" over and over again. The wait had created expectation in him and now that the day had finally arrived he couldn't contain his excitement. His exclamation reveals one of the aspects of marriage that sets it apart from other relationships—physical oneness.

This oneness is God-ordained as we see in Jesus' response to a question about divorce. He replied by pointing them back to God's original creative principle of marriage:

> *"'Haven't you read', he replied, 'that at the beginning the Creator 'made them male and female', and said, 'For this reason a man will leave his father and mother and be united to his wife, and the two will become one flesh'? So they are no longer two, but*

---

1. *It is not the intention of this book to take you through sexual practice as others can do this with far greater expertise than I can. You will find resource recommendations in the appendix, which will give you a good grounding in the practicalities of your future sex life. I highly recommend that you both read these resources, as for just one of you to do so is counterproductive. You both need to be on the same page or you will find conflict and disappointment.*

one flesh. Therefore what God has joined together, let no one separate'."

—Matthew 19:4-6 (NIV)

In marriage, there is a 'leaving;' a moving away from one's parents and childhood home to be united as a couple, becoming 'one flesh'. There is no doubt that 'one flesh' refers to the ultimate act of intimacy between a male and a female: their sexual union. Jesus is making it clear here that this is a godly act—it has his approval and is part of God's will and design for how we live our lives. He is the architect behind marriage and the sexual activity that goes with it. He has given us sex within the confines of marriage as a sign that we are no longer two but one, and of course, for our pleasure and enjoyment.

Yet the physical side of marriage is not solely about sex. Rather, it is about cultivating a lifestyle of love and affection which creates a deep sense of acceptance and belonging that then culminates in sex. Being 'one' is about both partners being fulfilled in who they are as individual parts of the whole. As we pursue this state of unity, we are drawn into a secure relationship where we are both able to trust the other's commitment to the relationship. We do not lose our personalities or individuality within this oneness, but in this place of entwining our lives with another in interdependency, we find the freedom and support to be our truest and best selves; through our union we create a place of rest for one another.

DEVELOPING A LIFESTYLE OF INTIMACY

At the moment of marriage, you make promises to each other. Perhaps your vows read something like this: "I promise before the Lord, that for better or worse, for richer or poorer, in sickness and in health, I will love you, cherish, help and comfort you, until death us do part." These promises are important. It is so easy just to say them and then forget them in moments of crisis or conflict or grief, but unless we incorporate these vows we made into our lives and make them part of who we are, they become meaningless.

Once when I was a guest speaker at a church, a man asked to see me. He was upset with his wife because she was feeling down and had become distracted from what they had both been involved with previously. He felt like she was no longer with him in what he was doing and was thinking of leaving her as he could not stand it anymore. It came up in the course of our conversation, however, that his wife's sister had died not too long ago. With only five minutes to advise him before we left, I asked him what he had promised his wife when they got married. He was able to quote their vows, "I will love you, cherish, help, and comfort you." I challenged him as to why he was not keeping those promises. He looked shocked, so I explained that his wife had lost her sister and needed him to support her in her grief. I encouraged him to buy some flowers on his way home, then tell her he was sorry for not being there for her, that he loved her, and wanted to help. Our paths crossed again some time later, and he confessed that while he had hated what I said to him, he had done as I suggested, and it had saved his marriage. His wife responded to his love and felt helped in overcoming the grief she had been feeling so alone in. Oneness had been restored in their relationship, and she was now able to reciprocate the love and care.

Cherishing one another—caring for each other's needs in both good and hard seasons—is a key part of our building intimacy in our relationship, as is affection. Affection can act as a thermometer of our love and oneness and is demonstrated through touch, hugs, and our sexual union.

The cooling of a physical connection in the marriage relationship is often precipitated by a neglect of communication. Maybe busyness has pushed aside date nights, work is stressful, or for whatever other reason you no have time for extended talking, listening, and connecting with each other. There is simply no longer any allowed space to share yourselves.

Neglecting foundational habits is not usually deliberate. It starts slowly, almost unnoticeably, and you are unaware that you have started to neglect the very principles that keep your relationship alive and active. Then you gradually begin to feel something has changed—you become aware that you have stopped touching, stopped kissing hello and goodbye, stopped holding hands and looking each other in the eye. You give curt answers to questions, get irritable, and become less and less interested in sexual encounters.

If we are honest, we know that these things will happen to all of us from time to time. We are, after all, human beings who have feelings and are often easily hurt or offended, especially under stress or when there is a lack of sleep. This is why we need to put our foundational habits in place and commit to practicing them. For Mary and me, some of these foundational habits have been holding hands, kissing goodbye when we part, spontaneous hugs, and not neglecting Monday which has been our day together for over fifty years. These things, among others, have kept our relationship strong throughout our entire marriage because we have prioritised keeping them alive, active, and polished—*Alive,* because you are not in a dead relationship, you are in a relationship which needs to be daily invested in; *Active,* because you are determined together not to give up doing the things that keep your relationship fresh; and *Polished,* because years of practice has caused them to become a well-established fixture in your lives. We've found that when we commit to keeping our foundational habits alive, active, and polished, our sex-life stays healthy.

In many ways sex is the ultimate indicator to how our oneness is going because it is, generally speaking, a measure of how well you are caring for one another. Sexual union is the expression of a life full of love and affection between two people whose lives have become bound up in each other in a covenant of pleasure given to us by God. It is a deeply joyful expression of intimacy between two people. But sometimes, past experience and unrealistic expectations rob us of the gift that sex was intended to be to our marriage.

MANAGING EXPECTATIONS

Sex is the most intimate aspect of marriage: nobody else knows what we do or how often we do it. However, it is not something that can be done automatically; the art of sexual union has to be learned. The problem is that we have images in our minds about what it should be like. These images have been planted in us through movies, magazines, books, pornography, and the general gossip and banter of what it means to be 'good in bed'. Much of what we see is false, and it sets us up for disappointment.

Movies and television often portray a couple ripping the clothes off each other, perhaps the man slamming the woman against a wall—but what we're watching is scripted and has no real passion attached to it; the actors are doing a job, not living a life. The problem is that we have become conditioned by such scenes as to what good sex is. It is quite natural that we want to live up to these expectations that have been logged into our minds. But these unrealistic and fanciful scenarios often rob us of true intimacy because they put the focus on our own needs and desires rather than on loving and pleasuring our partner. This often leads to one-way sexual fulfilment.

This self-focus is even more problematic for those who have been influenced by pornography. Pornography is an act; a performance intended to stimulate the senses. But these carefully staged scenes function like a drug; the more you view the more you want. It creates a completely one-sided and selfish compulsion with no consideration of another person's needs and satisfaction, and it is incompatible with a normal sexual relationship with a partner. It can even inhibit you from enjoying sex, leaving you unable to perform without the stimulation of visual images.

I remember a newly married couple coming to me with a problem. Before they married, he had watched a lot of pornography, and because his brain was so used to being stimulated by images, he had trouble performing sexually without them. His solution to this problem was to ask his wife to watch pornography with him and then re-enact it with him. The wife was upset by this. She had no interest in watching porn and wanted advice—my advice was simple: Stop watching it, and break the cycle! I encouraged him to stop all thoughts of using images as stimulation and for them to learn together what pleased them both. This took effort and commitment but eventually the cycle of pornographic stimulation that had gripped him was broken.

This disconnection from reality that media (and especially pornography) create, can be summed up by an article I read in a magazine. An ex-madam of a brothel was replying to a man who had written in to say that he only got what he needed when he visited a prostitute and that ordinary sex was boring and disappointing. She pointed out that when he was with a prostitute, it was purely professional and completely one-sided because the prostitute was in no way invested in her own satisfaction. It was all for her client; she was simply supplying a service. He was encouraged to reject the falsehood that sex with a prostitute was better and accept sex with any future partner as a two-way relationship, as what he was expressing prioritised only his own needs and satisfaction and would be of no help in establishing a future intimate relationship with a life-partner.

It is vital to the health of your oneness that you recognise the temptations you each face and the way in which your expectations have been shaped by outside influences. As a couple you need to be on the same page so that you can fully enjoy your sexual union the way God designed you to. One of the first ways that you do this is through *confession.*

If you are getting married and one of you has been or is involved with pornography or any other sexual deviance, this needs to come into the open. Such things should not remain a secret. One day they will inevitably be revealed, and if they have been deliberately concealed, it is usually with devastating consequences. Don't assume that because you are Christians you are immune to such things; the temptations are very real. With such easy access to pornography, we are regularly presented with the opportunity to view what we know is wrong—sometimes it even happens by accident.

I remember preparing a sermon in my office and wanted to do a bit of research online. For some reason, I put in a search for 'rubber'. I cannot remember why or the context, all I know is I did, and that the images that came up were designed to lead me into pornographic sites. Because of my past experience with pornography, I had to deliberately resist the urge to click on them. In all honesty, I had to shout out loud, "No!" and reach for the exit button. A moment of hesitation made me hover, but fortunately at that point I was reminded by the Holy Spirit of my youth and the consequences of continuing down that path. One click and I was out of that site. Even then it took me three or four days to keep those initial images at bay. Although the door had only opened a mere crack, temptation was a very powerful stimulant.

If you, like me, have been unduly influenced by unrealistic practices, the inner darkness needs to come into the light; it needs to be exposed—not to shame you, but to allow you to enter into the freedom of Christ. Jesus is the *light of the world*. He came to lead us out of darkness and into the light; out of sin into truth. Light exposes the deeds done in secret. People who are involved with sin find it difficult when those sins are revealed. But if you are involved with sin, any sin, not just sexual, the first step to breaking free is to deliberately expose it to the light.

This is what Jesus had to say:

> *"Light has come into the world, but people loved darkness instead of light because their deeds were evil. Everyone who does evil hates the light, and will not come into the light for fear that their deeds will be exposed. But whoever lives by the truth comes into the light, so that it may be seen plainly that what they have done has been done in the sight of God."*
>
> —JOHN 3:19-21 (NIV)

How do you come into the light? The bible tells us to 'confess', meaning 'to declare openly by way of speaking out freely'. In this way we open up our problem to others, not so that we can be condemned, but so that we can be forgiven, prayed for, and helped to overcome the problem (James 5:16).

Confession is the prerequisite for breakthrough. Our sexual sins and unrealistic sexual expectations need to be out in the open so that there are no hidden things that could create a barrier between you after you are married. A word of caution though: While these things may be difficult to hear, try not to respond in shock or hurt, as this will not help. The truth is that many fall into sexual sin and then become trapped and need help to escape.

Once things are out in the open a strategy has to be worked out to guard your sexual intimacy. The simplest way is to be accountable to one another and regularly ask one another questions, understanding that this is a battle and that victory takes perseverance and tenacity. It should be noted that these things are difficult to handle alone and the inclusion of a trusted third party who can guide you is almost essential. The reason for this is that when we have a problem, we can become resentful of our spouse checking in with how we are going and can end up saying things like, "You don't trust me, do you?" This question can be a cover-up, and may well mean that the problem is still there, but that you do not want to admit it because you feel ashamed.

We saw this happen with a couple where the husband was using his phone to engage in sexting. His wife hated it, and it was causing her much anguish. He had seen a counsellor and assured her the sexting had ended, yet when his wife asked to check his phone, he refused to show it to her. I don't know if he trotted out the old, "You don't trust me" line or not, but the truth was that his refusal meant he was almost certainly still involved. Continued openness and honesty help generate and safe-guard your trust in one another even when the problem has been overcome. If you are the one being held accountable, rather than being resentful, try to embrace any enquiry with openness, knowing that it is for your own good and the good of your relationship.

When looking for a third party to help you, find somebody you trust and make yourselves accountable to them as a couple, The people who came alongside you in your pre-marriage preparation are often a good option if they are available. I have done this for quite a few people and couples over the years and know from that experience that it is not easy to get out of the bad habits. It takes perseverance, love and grace, and there are many backward steps, but in the end, overcoming can and does happen.

I remember the pain of one man who was so bound by unrealistic sexual practices that he could not pursue a normal relationship with any, what he called, 'real women'. Under advice, he decided to take drastic action: total abstinence from all sexual internet viewing, masturbation, and dating. He was going to be celibate until he overcame his addiction.

As I and one other person who shared the task of holding him accountable spoke to him each week, you could see the agony written all over him. This thing had become a stronghold; it had him in a vice-like grip, and it needed breaking. This was why it was necessary for him to know that each and every week we would ask him how he was going. Even then, on occasions he failed, but we picked him up, dusted him down, forgave him, and prayed for him in Jesus' name, encouraging him to persevere. Eventually he did break the cycle; the stronghold was demolished and he never went back to his old ways—he even got married to a 'real woman'.

When you are trying to break a stronghold it's like a wrecking ball being pounded against a wall. It hits that wall many times and can look like it is doing no good at all, yet the truth is that the wall is being weakened with every hit—suddenly after many hits, a crack appears, and that crack then gets wider and wider until the wall collapses. If you will work together, you can confront the strongholds and unrealistic expectations that threaten your unity and create a healthy sexual relationship that is mutually satisfying.

Gaining a realistic expectation of your intimate life together is something that comes about as you learn and explore physical love together. It must be based on what each of you likes, and not what others say you should like. If one of you does not like something, then out of respect and love for your partner, don't do it. However, try not to make that judgement without trying. If you have tried and are still not happy, just don't do it, and cut that out of your intimate life. If you are the partner that wants to do something that your partner does not like, accept that and be the one who does not impose or demand that of your partner just because you want to do it. Always remember that this is intimacy with pleasure, not a competitive sport in which new goals and techniques need to be continually attained.

In establishing the pattern of your love life, information is key—not false, scripted information from the media, or what we call 'gutter information' in which people brag about their sexual encounters to their friends—you need to know what God's Word has to say on the subject. Paul was quite revolutionary concerning the relationship of male and female. In his time, patriarchy (male domination over women) was the order of the day. Men had accepted power over women and this would have also been true in terms of sex. This is reflected in Paul's statement in 1 Corinthians 7:4 when he says that a man has control over his wife's body; it belongs to him. What is completely contradictory to the culture of the time is Paul's assertion that the *husband's* body does not belong to him alone, but also to his wife. He is quite blunt about it; sex is for *mutual* pleasure and satisfaction. He tells *both husband and wife* that they should not deprive each other of sex except by mutual consent, and then only for a limited time and specific purpose (v. 5). He is spelling out that for Christians, sex is a mutual activity, exclusive and essential to their union, with equality built into it. What is true for one is true for the other.

One of the questions we often get asked in relation to not depriving one another is how frequently a couple should be having sex. There is no one right answer to this, because for each couple there are different circumstances. But the guiding principle as you determine what works for you is found in 1 Corinthians 7—abstinence from sexual relations is only to be by mutual agreement and for a set time and specific reason. In other words, you are going to need to communicate as a couple about what works for you in any given season.

We knew one couple who were in such high-pressure jobs that they found that the expectation and effort required to make love only added more pressure to their lives. They made the mutual decision that they would leave all sexual activity for when they were on holiday. Affection was still present in their relationship but sex was for holidays and then they allowed themselves to fully and freely enjoy this aspect of their relationship. They were concerned whether it was right or not to do this, but we reassured them that if they were both content and satisfied with this arrangement, then it was perfectly okay. Another couple only made love at the weekends; yet another couple made love every day. Work out your own patterns over time, and as long as it is mutual, then flow with it.

There will be times where a compromise may be necessary if you cannot reach an agreement. In these situations, you need to remember that your responsibility is always to put your partner's wellbeing first. But don't let pressure come from outside sources; there is no norm you have to adhere to. There are, however, some abiding principles:

Never engage in something that one of you does not like or want to do.

Never hurt one another.

Never talk to anybody else about what you do in your sex life unless it is to help or counsel others who are having difficulties or you are in need of counsel yourselves, and even then, only if you have both given consent.

I have used the expression numerous times, 'being on the same page'. However you get there, whether by reading the same books or discussing your expectations, desires, and any fears you might have regarding sex, this is necessary—even if you have already had sex prior to getting married. Seeking to truly understand one another in this area will be a good platform to build your future intimacy on and will lead you towards the ultimate goal of your sexual union: true oneness.

9

Money

Growing up in boarding schools not only limited my understanding of women, it also impacted how I related to money. We seldom had money of our own at school, and on the rare occasion that we did, it was very quickly spent in the 'tuck-shop'. Once I started working, I continued in the same manner—spend, spend, and spend. I paid little attention to how I was spending my money, frittering it away each week. Mary, on the other hand, was from a poor but stable family background where every penny was accounted for. As a result, she did not spend frivolously and was able to save when needed. Just as we had not understood how our gender differences and varying family cultures would create conflict, so too did we fail to see how our differing approaches to money would impact our relationship.

Different attitudes to money have a powerful impact on a relationship. Frankly, left unaddressed, your financial habits will erode trust and even have the potential to destroy your marriage. Money causes more disputes, more despair, more arguments, and more divorces than any other problem, except for infidelity. To avoid this, not only do you need to understand what I call your 'financial personalities', but just as you have worked to get on the same page sexually, you will also need to work to get on the same page financially, establishing the values and principles that will guide how you manage money.

UNDERSTANDING YOUR FINANCIAL PERSONALITY

Typically, people fall into one of two categories: they are either a saver, or a spender. In most marriages, both the saver and spender are represented—opposites really do attract! However, it is important to understand that neither of these personalities is intrinsically right or wrong, and each of them will bring both advantages and disadvantages to how you manage your money. What matters is that you don't dismiss your differences but learn to respect them, and that you work together to harness the strengths of both the saver and the spender.

Savers account for every spare penny, carefully putting money aside for a rainy day, or a specific purpose like a holiday or big-ticket item. For some, they don't even need a goal—they simply like to save! Sometimes this tendency to squirrel money away is driven by childhood experience. Perhaps their family was poor and there was never enough to eat, or they faced a family crisis like a parent losing their job or having to sell their house, fuelling a need for stability and security. For others, it's part of how they are wired; they were born a saver. This ability of the saver to curb unnecessary spending and put funds aside is a gift to your marriage—their discipline provides financial security for your future together. What savers need to guard against however, is stifling a spirit of generosity by continually blocking spending. That is not a problem that the spender has!

The spender is one of whom it is often said, "Money burns a hole in their pocket." It just goes and often cannot be accounted for. This, I confess, was me as a young man. My money seemed to disappear and I often did not even know what I had spent it on. At one point, it got so bad that I would run out of money halfway through the week and have nothing left to buy food with, even though I was in a well-paid job. Fortunately, I always knew that Mary's mum would feed me if I was desperate! What I now know, is that I wasted a lot of money which created a disadvantage when we married and needed money. Our early years could have been much more stable and enjoyable if I had known how to better manage my finances. If you are the spender, understand that your personality carries the most risk; at their worst, spenders have no control over spending, and they need the saver to keep them on the right track. But while the spender can sometimes be wasteful, they can also have a tendency to be extremely generous, getting great enjoyment from blessing other people and buying them gifts or taking them out.

Some good friends of ours demonstrate well how both financial personalities can benefit a marriage when their strengths are harnessed. This couple were in ministry and were never particularly well-paid, but despite this were able to buy their own home and be very comfortable in their retirement years because the saver had been careful with any surplus money that they did have, putting away small amounts into investment accounts as they were able. The interest that accrued over decades of saving was a tremendous blessing to them in their latter years. However, while they had prioritised saving, the saver hadn't been pushy in their approach. The spender had still been free to buy gifts, organise family holidays, and encourage generosity in their family. There had been conflict over the years when the spender wanted to spend more than the saver, but with hindsight, the spender was delighted and extremely grateful with the benefits the saver had achieved for them when it mattered.

The two personalities can clash badly if one seeks to dominate the other, yet the truth is that in the long run both greatly benefit a marriage, bringing balance to how a couple approaches their finances. The spender should never crush the saver's instincts, and the saver should respect the spender's desire to be generous. You can do this by freeing one another up with agreed checks and balances, for the benefit of your future together. These checks and balances will be shaped by your shared financial values and goals.

DEFINING YOUR FINANCIAL VALUES

As Christians, the first step in deciding how we will steward our money is to learn what God has to say on the matter and to then align our financial habits with the truths set out in his Word. These become the foundation upon which we set our goals, determine our priorities, and practically manage our household budget.

In the New Testament, we find six important principles for stewarding our financial resources: giving to everyone what you owe them; leaving no debt remaining outstanding; keeping yourself free from the love of money; generosity; being content with what you have; and serving God not money. In Romans 13:7-8, Paul establishes the first two principles when he says:

> *"Give to everyone what you owe them: Pay your taxes and government fees to those who collect them, and give respect and honour to those who are in authority. Owe nothing to anyone—except for your obligation to love one another. If you love your neighbour, you will fulfill the requirements of God's law."*

Paul is clear: *Give to everyone what you owe them*. This includes not only taxes but also any other bills we may generate through our lifestyle. However, he takes this principle further than just money, saying that we should give respect and honour to those who deserve them. If this becomes a principle for you as a couple, it will be the incentive for you to control what happens to your income and savings because you will not want to dishonour anyone by not being able to pay them on time.

This leads to the second of Paul's principles: *Let no debt remain outstanding*. What this means in practice will be interpreted in varying ways depending on your understanding of 'debt'. If, for instance, you take Paul's words literally, you will not even consider taking out a mortgage because it is an outstanding debt. However, if you take the position that the mortgage is covered by the value of the house, you may not consider this an outstanding debt because if need be, the property can be sold to pay any balance on the mortgage. For some, debt is any outstanding amount that cannot be repaid immediately, regardless of any future income. In this case, everything must be saved for before purchasing. For others, it is any amount that you cannot cover from the funds that will be available to you on the date the payment is due. If you hold the latter view, you will see it as permissible to take out a loan for a car because the repayments can be easily covered by future income, or the car can be sold to repay the loan if the income fails to materialise. *Is either position wrong?* That is for each person or couple to work out for themselves, but if you are to avoid a situation where you are unable to pay your essential expenses, you will need to have decided in advance what constitutes debt and commit to abide by this principle.

Sometimes debt is driven by materialistic desire—we want to be seen to be 'keeping up with the Joneses'. This is why it is important that we adhere to the third principle of financial stewardship, found in Hebrews 13:5: *Keep yourselves free from the love of money*. Money itself should never be the dream. I once knew a man who appeared to be poor. He rode a bike made up of bits he had found at the scrapyard and even saved odd shoes so that he could create new, albeit mismatched, pairs with them. Over the years, he had also refused to pay for flights for him and his wife to visit their daughter who was living overseas. So it was a great surprise to his family when he died to discover that he was not poor at all, but very well off, with an extensive portfolio of shares. This refusal to spend money could have been a case of loving money itself and enjoying watching it accumulate, but at the expense of something more.

Despite never having been particularly wealthy, I have an understanding of this. When we moved to New Zealand, the exchange rates were in our favour, and so, having sold our house back in the United Kingdom, we found ourselves with more money than ever before. Up until this point we had lived on a zero bank balance. We were earning, but by the time the next pay went into the bank we were just about back to zero. So, to have money in the bank was very new to us, and even after buying a house and car outright, we still had what to us was a lot of money in the bank. That was when I discovered the power of the bank balance. Suddenly I found myself wanting to guard that balance, and this stopped us from giving in the way we were used to. Once I realised what had happened, I resolved to never allow myself to fall into that trap again, but it took some effort to break free. It's a subtle trap that we can fall into—allowing a bank balance to give us the feeling of security. It is what money can provide that is important; otherwise, money itself has no purpose.

One of the things that can help keep our hearts free from the love of money is the fourth principle of maintaining a spirit of generosity throughout our lives: *Give and it will be given to you.* This exhortation is found in Luke 6:38, where we read, "the measure you use, it will be measured to you." If you use a teaspoon, then that is the measure you will receive back. If you use a bucket, you will be blessed accordingly. It is not a formula, but it is a principle. If you bless others, you will be blessed in like manner.

I well remember a situation where this principle was exploited. A man owed fees to the Christian school his children were attending, but since he did not have the full amount, he was going to pay what he had and try to pay the rest later. Before he paid the money, however, he received a leaflet through the post about a church that was raising funds for their building project. The leaflet came with a promise that misquoted the verse in Luke 6:38. "Give us your money and God will multiply it for you," was the message. The man thought, *If I give money to this project, perhaps God will multiply it and then I will be able to give more to the school.* He came to me very down in mood because it just did not happen.

Had God let him down? No, he had forgotten that the Bible also says: "Give to everyone what you owe them" (Romans 13:7). Apart from that, the message of the leaflet was wrong—expecting blessing in return for our giving is not a formula, but a principle to live by. This principle for living a generous life is found in this Scripture:

> *"Our desire is not that others might be relieved while you are hard pressed, but that there might be equality. At present your plenty will supply what they need so that in turn their plenty*

will supply what you need. Then there will be equality, as it is written: 'He who gathered much did not have too much, and he who gathered little did not have too little'."

—2 Corinthians 8:13-15 (NIV)

If we are to be generous people who avoid debt, then we need to learn the next principle: *Be content with what you have, and live within your means.* To live within our means implies that we need to control our income by living in the reality of what we have rather than what we do not have. We must budget for day-to-day expenses according to the amount of money we have coming in each month. We need a financial plan! In reality, the less you earn, the more you need to have a plan. One of the most crucial things you can do as you embark on your life together is to set a budget and stick to it. The Bible reminds us that godliness with contentment brings great gain (1 Timothy 6:6). Just as the saver brings long-term benefits to your family, so too will learning to be content and live within the boundaries of your budget.

As you create your financial plan, there are some practical things that are worth considering. The first of these is that you need to identify your actual income and expenditure. Do not leave anything out of potential outgoings, no matter how small. It is essential that you account for not only your regular and fixed payments, but also your variable ones if you are to control your money and it not be the other way around! Once you have identified these things, there are various ways of tracking and managing your finances (some of which you will find in the recommended resources in the appendix). The important thing is that you find a system that works for you and serves your vision. It has to fit you—you can adopt somebody else's way of budgeting, but make sure you can keep it up consistently.

Secondly, if you want to save, separate your savings from your everyday bank accounts. So often we think we cannot save, that we need every cent and there is no slack to enable us to save. This was true for Mary and me, or so we thought. But the following story will illustrate that we could save;

we just did not know how to go about it:

In the United Kingdom we received a 'family allowance' from the government for our two children. The record of this was in a payment book which we took to the post office every week when we went to withdraw the allowance. At the time, this allowance felt essential to our weekly budget. The government then changed the system and began paying the family allowance directly into a bank account once a month. We thought this very inconvenient, considering we would now have to go to a bank rather than our local post office, to draw the money out. For some reason, we gave the government a savings account number we rarely used, and promptly forgot about it. You see, we thought we needed this money, but in reality we had just gotten used to having it. When we remembered the payments, we discovered hundreds of pounds which we had saved without even trying! We did not realise our capacity to save until those funds were separated from our day-to-day money.

As you seek to come together in your finances, there is one final principle that undergirds them all: *We serve God, not money.* Valuing money over God can lead us into ruin and destruction. As Paul cautions, "The love of money is a root of all kinds of evil" (1 Timothy 6:10, NIV). Paul is not saying that money itself is evil, but that the love of it is because of what that love is capable of causing us to do—it can even be the reason we walk away from faith. Before warning us of the danger of money, Paul tells us: "Some people, eager for money, have wandered from the faith and pierced themselves with many griefs" (v. 10). If we do not wish to be pierced by the griefs of money, we must determine whether God or money is our master, because Jesus is clear that we cannot serve them both (Matthew 6:24).

∿

How these principles are outworked in practice will look different for every couple. There are, however, certain things that you must avoid in order to safeguard your trust in one another. Trust (the firm belief in the reliability, truth, or ability of someone or something) is essential in any marriage. One of the things that will instantaneously damage your trust in one another is secret spending.

To state the obvious, secret spending is expenditure that your partner knows nothing about—and that you *want* them to know nothing about! We knew a wife who discovered, after many years of marriage, that her husband had a serious gambling problem. He had kept their bank statements away from the family, and so it was quite by accident that she discovered the deception. She trusted her husband and had no idea this had been going on. In one moment, her belief in his reliability and the truth of his words was gone. This deceit was possible because at some time in the early stages of their marriage, the wife had allowed her husband to exclusively take over the control of their family accounts, with no accountability. She used her credit and bank cards to manage their household expenses, but behind their normality was a dark secret.

Committing to openness around all family income and expenditure is not about a lack of trust; it is about guarding the trust that exists between you. There is a vulnerability within each one of us when we wield power with no accountability, and financial transparency helps protect you from temptation. Mary and I both know what our income is and we both know what we spend because bank and credit card statements are open to both of us. The only exceptions are birthdays, Christmas and anniversaries, and even then, budgets are set, and after those events we both know what has been spent. There are checks and balances to ensure we control our money instead of the other way around.

In addition to safeguarding ourselves against secret spending, Mary and I have also made it a point to avoid 'go-it-alone' purchasing. This is where one partner purchases major items without the knowledge of their other half. You may have different definitions of what constitutes a major item—for you, it might be the cost of the item, or it may be the significance of its place in your home. Again, this is why defining your values, priorities, and setting a budget is so important. It will help you avoid many of the trials and tribulations that can arise around the control of money.

Taking the time to have these conversations is one of the most important things you can do for your marriage. Money has such a strong bearing on what we can and cannot do with our lives, and managing it well will not only protect your marriage, it will put you in a better position to withstand hard times and unforeseen events while also allowing you to enjoy the things that money affords us.

10

Faith

I entered marriage as a new Christian. I was immature in spiritual things, and often attended things like prayer meetings only because Mary was going. Left to my own devices, I probably would not have bothered. Mary, on the other hand, came from a deeply-rooted Christian family with a strong heritage of faith, and without her determination to follow God, I may not have ended up a church leader as I did. I faced a choice in those early days to go along with Mary or hold back. At first I chose to go to church because Mary was going, but later I went because I too wanted to grow in my walk with God. I had a willingness and openness to God, and gradually I matured in faith. Later in our married life, it was me who contributed to Mary's spiritual growth, helping her as she adjusted from some of the restrictions her traditional Christian background had instilled in her. Ultimately, we grew in spiritual maturity *together*.

When we talk about our faith, there are two aspects we need to consider—our individual relationship with God and our relationship with him as a couple. Both are important; if one of those is out of kilter the balance of our marital relationship can be become lopsided or even damaged.

A friend of ours found herself in this situation. She had met her husband at church and he had displayed all the attributes of a Christian man—at least, until after the honeymoon. On their first Sunday back home, she got ready for church and called to her husband that it was time for them to leave, only to have him inform her that he would no longer be attending church with her. He had her, so there was no need to go on pretending that he was a Christian. From that moment on, he did everything he could to frustrate her faith. This led to many years of deep anxiety for this woman who was committed to walking with God and yearned for her husband to join her. Spiritually, this couple was 'unequally yoked', and it created a limp in their relationship, affecting much more than their spiritual togetherness. Eventually, after some thirty plus years, he did surrender his life to Christ, but there was much heartache in the intervening years.

To walk well with God together, we first need a personal relationship with him, because it is not couples who receive salvation but individuals. In a godly marriage, we each still pursue our own relationship with God, but we are also brought together to serve him as a team. To do this, we do not necessarily need to share the same level of spiritual maturity, but we do need a commitment to walk together in faith.

THE PRIORITY OF PRAYER

So what does it look like to walk with God as a couple? There are obvious things, such as belonging to the same church family, attending and serving together, and giving, but one of the things that Mary and I have found most helps us to walk in faith together is prayer.

Mother Teresa said, "The family that prays together stays together, and if they stay together, they will love one another as God has loved each one of them. And works of love are always works of peace." These are wise words. When we pray, we present ourselves to God to seek his will and to gain his strength, and when we do that together, our differences are put aside as we focus on what he is saying. The way that we relate to one another becomes based not on our desires, but his, and this brings a stability to our relationship that enables us to stay the course no matter what is thrown at us.

Praying as a couple is an opportunity to bring before God all aspects of your relationship. It is an opportunity to express what each of you are thankful for, to identify areas where you may be struggling, and to recognise any danger that may be pressing in from outside of your marriage. If God is the source of life for us as individuals, then he is also the source of life for us as couples. When we learn to prayerfully depend upon him as our source, our love for him and for one another will increase, as will the peace Mother Teresa spoke of.

Over the years, whenever we've tackled the subject of prayer in our pre-marriage courses and counselling, we have always been surprised that wives nearly always expect and want their husbands to take the lead spiritually, especially when it comes to family prayer. One wife stated it very clearly, "It is his job to lead us to God and I wish he would just get on with it." It is almost as though there is a spiritual instinct for wives to want their men to be taking ownership of leading and maintaining this aspect of their lives together. To be taking spiritual responsibility for his family is one of the pinnacles of godly manliness.

When the apostle Peter taught on how men are to relate to their wives, he said that they were to treat them with 'understanding' (1 Peter 3:7). The Greek word translated 'understanding', means 'knowledge or knowing'. If you want to *understand* your wife, you must take the time to *know* her. Truly knowing her allows you to honour her for who she is, not just for what you want her to be. This understanding is relevant to prayer, because failing to know our wives and to respect them as equals hinders a man's ability to maintain a good relationship with God. This is what we see playing out in the book of Malachi where we read:

> *You flood the Lord's altar with tears. You weep and wail because he no longer looks with favor on your offerings or accepts them with pleasure from your hands. You ask, "Why?" It is because the Lord is the witness between you and the wife of your youth. You have been unfaithful to her, though she is your partner, the*

> *wife of your marriage covenant. Has not the one God made you? You belong to him in body and spirit . . . So be on your guard, and do not be unfaithful to the wife of your youth.*
>
> —Malachi 2:13-15 (NIV)

This passage teaches us that a man's effectiveness in prayer is directly related to how he treats his wife. Malachi tells of a man who is weeping because he can no longer get through to God; his prayers and sacrifices are all to no avail. *Why?* Because he has dishonoured and been unfaithful to his wife.

This responsibility on husbands throughout Scripture may be why women carry such desire to see them lead their families in prayer. However, the reality is that either of you can take spiritual responsibility for coming before God and praying together. What really matters is that it happens!

But sometimes, we simply don't know where to start. Fortunately, the Bible gives us some clues about how we can establish prayer as a foundational practice in our lives. Firstly, it tells us not to give up praying (Luke 18:1). Now this is sometimes easier said than done, because the truth is, it's easy to forget to pray. It often starts with the occasional 'too tired' or 'too busy' as an excuse for not suggesting that we pray together about something, but over time prayer can become sporadic, and often ends up with us not praying at all. This is why it is often good to determine who will take responsibility for ensuring these times of prayer happen. Another encouragement Scripture gives us is to be thankful on every occasion (1 Thessalonians 5:17-18). Thankfulness is a powerful counter to negativity, anxiety and fear, because giving thanks is a statement that we will trust God in every situation and circumstance. The Bible also teaches us to ask God for the wisdom that we need (James 1:5).

I well remember, as a young Christian, reading the story of Solomon. One night, God came to him and said, "Ask for whatever you want me to give you" (2 Chronicles 1:7, NIV). Solomon's answer was generated by the task that was before him. It was as though he knew that to succeed, he needed something that could only come from God, so he replied, "Give me wisdom and knowledge, that I may lead this people, for who is able to govern this great people of yours?" (v. 10). As a young man reading that, I decided wisdom was something I also wanted, so I asked God to give it to me and have desired it all my life from that moment on. This was long before I discovered that James told us that if we lack wisdom then we should ask God and it will be given us.

One of the ways that I define wisdom, is being able to 'see'. When we marry, we make a commitment to seek the welfare of our spouse and to bless them. But the problem, as we have discovered, is that often we are 'seeing' only from our own limited perspective, and so we fail to understand what they need. God can give us the insights we lack; he can give us wisdom. In a marriage, when we are able to see our partner and our circumstances from God's perspective, we are able to pray for them effectively, discern the way forward, and find solutions. Seek wisdom and knowledge for one another—that will bring understanding, and understanding will bring a continued peace between you, enabling your love to grow through every circumstance.

But as well as providing principles that should undergird our prayer life, Scripture also gives us a model for prayer.

A MODEL FOR PRAYER

When the disciples asked Jesus to teach them how to pray, he gave them what is now known as 'The Lord's Prayer.'

> *"Our Father in heaven,*
> *hallowed be your name,*
> *your kingdom come,*
> *your will be done,*
> *on earth as it is in heaven.*
> *Give us today our daily bread.*

And forgive us our debts,
  as we also have forgiven our debtors.
And lead us not into temptation,
but deliver us from the evil one."
—MATTHEW 6:9-13 (NIV)

It is interesting that before Jesus introduces this prayer, he tells them that the Father knows what we need even before we ask. That doesn't mean we do not need to ask—it simply means that we can ask in confidence. Jesus wanted them, and us, to seek after God for ourselves, and one of the ways we do this is through prayer. The model that Jesus lays out for us gives us five areas in which we need to continually seek God.

The prayer begins with the acknowledgement that God is a Father to us, and a request that his name be 'hallowed' (v. 9). It is a reminder to us that not only do we approach God as his beloved children, but that we are *to seek his renown*, showing concern for his reputation. By anchoring us in the truth that God is our Father, Jesus is inviting us to come before him with great expectation. Just as we know that good earthly fathers want what is good for their children, we know our Heavenly Father does too. This does not mean we always get what we want, but it reminds us that we can trust his heart toward us. Equally, because we are his children, we will care for the 'family name'. How we conduct ourselves reflects on our Father, and so we prayerfully commit ourselves to him, asking him to help us treat others well and enable us to live in such a way that he is glorified.

As part of this desire to represent him well, *we seek his will*, asking that his kingdom come and his purposes be realised in our lives—in marriage, in our children, in our churches, and beyond that, in our city and country, and in the nations of the world (v. 10). To understand God's will we need to be regularly reading and absorbing his Word so that we have the ability to recognise and discern what he is saying to us in our times of prayer. This knowledge of his Word helps us to align our family life with his will and reflect the ways of his Kingdom to all those around us in the hope that they, too, will also want to become his children.

God then invites us *to seek him for our daily bread*, asking him to provide what we need for each day and season (v. 11). Our need may be for a job, or healing, or guidance, or help in overcoming adversity . . . Again, because he is our Father, we can be confident that he cares about whatever needs we have.

We also need to regularly *seek forgiveness* and to check our hearts to see whether we are harbouring offence or bitterness (v. 12). Unforgiveness is a horrible barb that can dig deep into our personalities and warp our view of those around us. For peace to exist in our marriages we must determine to keep short accounts with one another and not hold on to grudges. My personal stand is that I will not be offended by anyone, with the ambition that I will not offend anyone else. That is a hard place to be sometimes, yet in prayer I can overcome offence by quickly forgiving those who may have hurt or offended me.

And finally, we *seek protection* from the temptations of this life which can destroy us, and deliverance from the evil one who seeks to lead us into those temptations (v. 13). There are any number of things that cause us to stumble in this life, which is why we must continually pray for one another, asking God to make us steadfast in the face of temptation. I once faced a situation where a young lady told me that she had fallen in love with me. The temptation was real, and I felt immediately drawn into its web. My marriage was on the line, as was my relationship with my children and my ministry. I had promised that I would be faithful to Mary all of my life, so I walked away and told that lady that I could never be alone with her again. If I walked into a room and she was by herself, I would walk back out. I prayed that God would deliver me from temptation and enable me to respond to this threat to my wife, family, and ministry. Prayer gave me the strength to resist, and I praise God that this was a habit for me.

Prayer connects us to the power of God, protecting us as the Holy Spirit brings to mind the truth by which we are called to live. Pray together for your life and family. Pray separately for one another, and when and if you have children, don't neglect to pray for them every day of their lives.

Prayer should be front and centre of our married lives because prayer brings God into the centre of our marriage. But I want to offer a word of caution about rigid and inflexible expectations as you seek to establish a foundation of prayer in your marriage. Don't create 'faith laws' that have no real scriptural basis. Grace rather than law must govern your spiritual life together. Grace is undeserved favour toward one another, while law is a rigid framework that can become crippling. I have seen too many couples and children struggling with man-made rules—*Do this and don't do that; Dress like this, especially on a Sunday; You must pray at this particular time of the day; Read this many chapters of the Bible.*

Your walk with God is not based on law but a relationship filled with grace. Your family life needs to be based on the same—it should be natural and easy, an everyday part of who you are, a recognition of the truth that God is always with you and that just as you are part of his family, he is part of yours. Take this relationship seriously, but also enjoy God and one another as he intended.

PART FOUR

After the Wedding

11

Marriage Check-up

We had come to the end of our marriage preparation sessions with one couple when the thought occurred to me that we should offer them a six-month check-up. This was not something we had ever suggested before—couples got engaged, and when we offered marriage preparation nobody ever turned it down, but once they were married, unless they asked for help, we assumed everything was alright. Because of the relationship we had built up over the six weeks we spent preparing them for marriage, many couples did reach out to us when they encountered problems and needed advice, *but a deliberate six-month check-up?* This was a new idea. There was no particular reason why I thought this couple needed one; it was a straightforward, unexpected prophetic insight that has subsequently borne much fruit.

The thought behind it was that there have been numerous occasions in our years of marriage counselling where we've found one partner is satisfied with an aspect of their life together, but unbeknown to them, their partner is feeling quite the opposite and is struggling with the very thing the other thinks is going well. For instance, one partner may be organising how they will manage their financial affairs and is enthusiastically putting a plan in place, unaware that their spouse isn't comfortable with certain aspects of what they are doing and for whatever reason, doesn't feel able to say so. The problem is usually simple: Our experience tells us that the partner who is taking the lead on a particular issue is not proactively asking for or listening to their partner's views and is therefore likely oblivious to their frustrations.

When these issues are not exposed and dealt with, they create further frustrations which in time lead to resentment. Resentment then typically causes one partner to simply give up, and when that happens, the result is disunity in that particular area. Repeat this in too many areas of your relationship and eventually you have an unhappy marriage. This is why it's important to identify any areas of difficulty before they become an entrenched habit.

But sometimes it's hard to ask one another how we're really doing. And even when we take the time to ask, we don't necessarily get the full story. We often temper our answers to accommodate our spouse—perhaps we don't want to hurt their feelings, or, if we've found them to be defensive in the past, we'll take that into account when deciding how much to share with them.

These are some of the reasons we began making six-month check-ups available, and to our surprise, the offer was enthusiastically taken up by every couple we presented this option to. What the check-up achieved, was to expose areas that needed a little correction in a safe and non-confrontational manner. The uncovering of these problems that were small but given time would have become large and entrenched, usually avoided the need for major intervention down the track.

One of the problems we faced as we started doing these check-ups was how to ask a series of very personal questions without making anyone feel embarrassed or uncomfortable. It seemed awkward to ask a couple: "Are you fulfilled when making love?" when they were both in the room. *Who was going to answer first? Would the one answering second be willing to say if they felt differently, or would they just keep quiet?*

For the check-up to succeed, we needed to find a way for each partner to give an honest appraisal of how well they thought the marriage was going. We also needed to identify the particular frustrations in each new partnership. By isolating the problems they faced, we could avoid spending time on areas that needed no correction. To facilitate all of this we created what we call 'The Marriage Health Indicator' to help us get a true reading on how a couple was doing.

MARRIAGE HEALTH INDICATOR

The *Marriage Health Indicator* is a survey designed to ascertain how well a married couple is doing in the following areas: communication, prayer, sex, money, personal contentment, and affection. Eight positive statements are given about each of these areas, which each spouse indicates their level of agreement with by using a number from zero to three. Zero means that the statement is not true for them at all, whereas a three indicates that they are in full agreement with it. So, if you are only partly in agreement you might put a one or two. For the indicator to work effectively, the participants need to fill it in at the same time and answer the questions as quickly as possible. It is their instinctive answer, not an over-thought one, that is needed to get an accurate picture. Another way that we get a correct understanding of where things sit in each area is through the repetitiveness of the statements. We've found that having to answer the same statement subtly reframed numerous times helps to confirm an individual's true position.

Once each spouse has completed the survey, we add up their responses, giving a maximum score of 24 for each area. As we assess the results, we're not only looking for where potential problems lie, but also where there might be communication issues. For example, if in the area of affection, one partner has put all zeros and the other has put all threes, we know that there's not just a problem there, but that they are not talking and being honest about it with each other.

The highest overall scores reflect the strongest aspects of a couple's marriage, while the lowest indicate the weakest. Noone needs a perfect score to consider their marriage successful. For the vast majority of couples, there will always be stronger and weaker areas in their life together—it just helps to know what they are. The assessment is not about getting a perfect score. Asking perfection of our spouse is setting standards that can never be reached and will therefore always lead to disappointment for us and a heavy burden for them. We have to accept that neither of us is, or ever will be, perfect. However, if we know where the vulnerabilities and problems lie, we can seek to do better for the sake of our spouse and our marriage.

When we were developing the *Marriage Health Indicator*, both Mary and I, and a newly married couple who we were working with, Andrew and Liz, trialled this questionnaire for ourselves. Andrew and Liz scored a perfect score in all areas—which was more than Mary and I did! This did not mean that Mary and I had problems, nor did it necessarily mean that Andrew and Liz didn't. It also wouldn't have helped to compare ourselves with Andrew and Liz. The goal is not to achieve a perfect score but to uncover any areas of concern to you as a couple. This is an important lesson to keep in mind as you assess your own relationship dynamics. You are not competing with anyone else's marriage—you are seeking to optimise your own unique union.

This is why, whether you use the *Marriage Health Indicator* or adopt a more informal approach to checking in with each other about the health of your relationship, there are some important principles to observe.

PRINCIPLES TO ABIDE BY

There is always the potential, when identifying weaknesses and honing in on areas of our relationship that need strengthening, for conversations to be divisive rather than healing. Because of this, if at all possible, it is best to *undertake this process with a trusted third party*, a mentor who can steer you through it.

Imagine what would happen if you did the assessment with just the two of you and you found yourself in the position of one couple we counselled who gave the opposite scores to the statement: I enjoy making love. The husband had scored this as 3, while his wife had written a zero. The husband was initially shocked, because he so enjoyed his sexual encounters with his wife. But his shock quickly turned to doubt in his own ability to satisfy his wife. He simply didn't know how to respond or how to go about finding out why his wife, who he adored, felt so differently to him. Because we were there, we were able to gently draw out why she had put a zero. It turned out that things were not as dire as they seemed, and all that was needed was an attitude adjustment on his part. The problem was that he was not thinking about his wife enough, and he needed to put a little more effort into focusing on her needs when they made love.

Could they have sorted through those feelings if we had not been with them? If they had the right attitude, then yes—but more often than not, a person's first response is to be defensive, which then makes it difficult to get to the root of the problem. If you are going to evaluate your marriage on your own, you need to vigorously apply three rules in order to succeed, the first of which is what we have just mentioned: *You cannot be defensive.*

The big problem with self-defence is that it shuts down the discussion because it requires the other person to either defend themselves or give in and admit they were wrong. If you are to solve a relationship problem it is essential that you accept what is being said as true for the person saying it.

Let's look at a hypothetical example. Your partner has placed a zero on the statement: My views are heard and considered by my partner. You have scored it a 3. Your initial reaction will likely be to defend your score. *Your partner must have somehow misunderstood you. There's no way that a zero is justifiable.* You've already concluded that it's not your problem, it's theirs.

It may well be true that you think you are a good listener, but your partner's zero simply means that they are not convinced you are. The correct way to approach this problem is to accept that you are not listening in a way that makes your spouse feel heard and understood and to ask how you can do better. The conversation might go something like this:

"Wow I put a three and you put zero. Why do you feel that way?"

"Because I do not feel that you understand my point of view. You listen and then move back to what you are thinking as if what I said has no relevance."

"I am sorry you feel that way. I do want you to know I am listening. How can I help communicate that I have heard and do understand? What will convince you?"

"Why not repeat back to me what you think I have said and mean. Then I can tell you if you are right. If we are making a decision, check that I agree rather than presuming you have heard and understood my viewpoint. Then I will feel part of the decision and I will do the same with you."

As you set aside your defensiveness and ask questions that seek to uncover how your partner feels, you will be better able to resolve the differences you are facing. The other thing that you must do is to *always accept your partner's score*.

One of the other things that can happen when we're trying to get on the same page in an area of our marriage is that we become anxious to make our own perspective heard. We're intimately aware of our own motivations and goals and can find ourselves shaping our words in order to secure the outcome we're hoping for. The intensity of our tone and gestures can cause our partner to feel like our mind is already made up and that there is little point in offering their thoughts. *The result?* They don't feel listened to.

It's important to accept at face value how your spouse has scored their answers without trying to bring them round to your point of view. If you have put a 3 and they've chosen zero—or vice versa—accept that there is a problem that needs correcting and work with them to find an approach that will work for you both. Even if you've scored similarly, you would do well to see how you could continue to grow in that area of your relationship. To do this effectively, you'll need to be willing to change your motivation. Rather than being driven by your own goals, your primary motivation must be the wellbeing of your spouse. When their welfare is your goal, not only will you accept and seek to understand their position, you'll also be careful in how you do so.

This is our final 'rule': *There are to be no comments of disapproval, censure, or blame as you navigate these conversations.* Avoid saying things like, "You just don't get it, do you?" or, "I see that went straight over your head," or "I wish you could see what I see!" These kinds of negative comments convey to the other that you see your position as superior, and it will shut down constructive discussion about what each of you are thinking, feeling, and experiencing. If in the heat of the moment you realise you've made such a comment, simply apologise and rephrase your words so that your spouse feels affirmed.

∼

We recommend that you check in using something like the *Marriage Health Indicator* around the six-month mark, and then repeat it after a year if you feel it is necessary. Undertaking such a process early on in the marriage helps to correct any issues before they become entrenched and complicated to solve. But it is also a useful tool at any stage of a marriage. A couple who had been married with children for many years came to us for help after something had happened that had impacted their relationship. We gave them the survey to fill out, and their results told us that, up until this point, they had had a sound marriage with no real problems. The issue had simply arisen because of the circumstances they were navigating. Working with us enabled them to put the situation into context. It allowed them to see that their marriage was, overall, healthy—a small correction was all that was needed. If the problem had not been addressed, however, it could have continued to fester and become a major rift over time.

Every marriage needs regular maintenance; this reality should never be viewed as a negative. It is natural to evaluate and work on your marriage and make changes as you grow together and navigate different seasons of your life. Making space to assess the health of your relationship will always be time well-invested as you seek to value one another and the union God has given you.

12

Then Came the Children

One of the most dramatic changes that will happen in your married life is the arrival of children. If you're reading this as part of your pre-marital preparation or are enjoying the early years of your marriage, the topic of kids may feel a little out of place here. But given that the vast majority of couples do go on to have children, it is wise to give some advance consideration to what will likely be the single most disruptive occurrence in your married life. That's not to say that their arrival is unwelcome or negative—on the contrary, for most couples the addition of children is very much desired and planned for. But it is a disruption nonetheless. Your lifestyle will change, your sleep interrupted, your freedom curtailed, to say nothing of the responsibility of nurturing and guiding a new life. This is one of the times where you will need to pay careful attention to the dynamics of your marriage relationship, regularly checking in with one another, and making the necessary changes to continue nurturing your oneness in this new stage of your life together.

The subject of children is a discussion that needs to be had even before you get married, and the question of whether or not both of you want children should be answered prior to making this commitment to one another. Everything is fine if you are both happy with having children, but if one of you has strong feelings about when or if you even want to have children that are different to the other's and these have not been made clear, the stage is set for significant conflict. This is another important area of your marriage where you will need to communicate and work together to be on the same page—not only about having children, but also about how you will raise them.

PLANNING FOR A FAMILY

Few things are more emotive than wanting a child, and for most couples, there comes a point in time when a deep longing to have a baby pushes its way into their hearts. We have an instinctive desire to reproduce—it's a part of our human nature—and once awakened, although we may put it off for a while, we can never quite eliminate a baby from our thinking. Even when we consider the implications of having children—the costs, the inconvenience of not being able to do what we like when we like, or even the sleepless nights we may see others going through—it changes nothing.

But sometimes, even though we both want children, we're not working to the same timetable. Let's consider for a moment the situation where one partner suddenly develops a deep longing for a baby, but the other isn't there yet. If you are the one who isn't quite ready, accept the validity of your spouse's desire. This desire for children is an unbidden, often irrational and unexpected yearning that cannot simply be dismissed; it seems to come from deep within, and once started, is almost impossible to stop. That's not to say you have to start trying for a baby then and there, but acknowledging and honouring how your spouse is feeling will help to avoid tension and to maintain your togetherness.

Equally, if you are the one in whom this desire for a baby has surfaced and is deepening, realise that this may well be a shock for your partner, especially if you have previously planned for a baby in say, five years or so. Whatever you do, do not reject this desire for a baby within yourself or your partner by saying that it is just not in the plan at the moment. Be prepared to change the plan! Talk and pray it through, and come to a mutual understanding of how to move forward.

You must also prepare for the possibility that sometimes trying to conceive does not go as expected. While this was not our experience, I have seen the frustration of couples who struggle; it is painful and all-consuming. No matter how long it takes, the desire for a baby never seems to go away. Friends of ours spent nine years trying to have a baby and when they had all but given up, suddenly found out they were pregnant. To see the joy after nine years of struggle was wonderful. And once the first baby came, a second quickly followed, and then a third baby made an appearance. If you find yourselves in this situation, you will need to be intentional about protecting your marriage and caring for one another's hearts. The value of your relationship is not diminished if you are unable to have biological children, so continue to invest in it.

We all have a mental picture of what it will look like to start a family. We look forward to hearing the baby's heartbeat, to seeing them for the first time at our scans, to finding out whether it's a boy or girl. At each step, excitement grows and anticipation builds as you start thinking about names, shopping for clothes, decorating baby's room, and so on. Grandparents join us in this excitement, offering up advice along the way.

Yet in the midst of all these wonderful things, there can also be difficulties in starting a family. Some agonise because they cannot conceive, while others struggle with their health during pregnancy—experiencing morning sickness, cramps, and complications. It's not always this way though. My Mary did not have one day of sickness with either of our children. She was, as they say, 'disgustingly healthy' and vibrant throughout both pregnancies. Whatever situation you find yourself in, know that the sacrifices are worth it—having a baby is a wonderful thing! This new addition will undoubtedly bring big changes to your life and relationship though, and how you adapt, handle, and support each other through this time is vital for the ongoing welfare of both yourselves and your marriage, and by extension, your future children.

MAINTAINING YOUR CONNECTION

The transition from being a couple to a family shifts the way you operate, but not who you are as a couple. The responsibility of parenting does not fall to one of you with the other playing a support role; the responsibility rests within the relationship as you jointly take on the task of parenting this new person. For this reason, maintaining the closeness of your connection as a couple is important. Not only is your unity vital to the ongoing health of your marriage, but also to the welfare, security and development of your baby as they grow from being a baby to a child and from a child to an adult.

From the outset, you must understand that the objective of parenting is not childhood but adulthood. Yet childhood is pivotal in producing a well-balanced adult. Your responsibility is to train your children to not only stand secure in our changing world, but to contribute to its ongoing development and security. The Bible puts the task of parenting in a very succinct way in Proverbs 22:6 when it tells us, "Train up a child in the way he should go; even when he is old he will not depart from it" (ESV). This verse teaches us that childhood is the training ground for adulthood, and that a child's tutors (that is, their parents) have the task of guiding and shaping them to this end. Certainly others will help you, grandparents, aunts, uncles, friends and teachers—it takes a village as they say—but the responsibility lies with you as a couple.

I do not mean to make this sound like a 'job' or an onerous task. It is so much more than that because it involves a deep-seated love that never goes away. When I first saw my children, I fell madly in love with them. I had loved the idea of them from the moment we first knew they were coming, but once I saw them and held them in my arms, I knew I loved them with all my being. I still do. They may be in their fifties now, but it makes no difference. Mary and I love them, want the best for them, pray for them daily, and continue to encourage and help them in any way we can.

Yet the truth is that we were always going to have to let them go.

Right from the start they were destined to head out into the world and live their own lives and have their own families. We wanted our children to be well-equipped and prepared for this independence from us, able to conduct themselves well in their interactions with the people around them. For this to be possible, we had to model it for them; we had to live the way that we hoped that they would when they moved into adulthood.

Have a look at the families you know with adult children. You will find that they generally reflect their parents in the way they behave. Their manners, politeness, care, and generosity are also in their parents—sometimes they even follow them into the same profession. There is assimilation that goes on as you raise your children even without you realising, so be intentional about the culture you create in your home. How you prioritise one another and your marriage is an important part of this intentionality.

For most couples, children are the inevitable result of married life, and having them will bring significant changes to your relationship. Your focus can no longer be exclusively on each other; it must also be on your children who are dependent on you to care and provide for them until you release them into adulthood. There is, however, one other inevitable: one day you will be on your own again as a couple. It won't quite be like it was when you first married because your children are still your children and they will continue to return home—maybe they'll even bring their laundry! But just like ours did, your children will go off to university or into employment and eventually permanently leave you to set up their own homes. In time, they may get married and have children of their own. Yes, eventually you too will become 'empty nesters'.

For many couples, this stage of married life can come as quite the shock. If their lives have been centred around their children, once they are on their own again, they find they have forgotten how to relate as a couple and need to find their path together again. Sadly, not all manage to do this. This is why it is important to maintain your connection as a couple during your parenting years. You need to guard your time alone without the kids; you need to keep dating. Make the most of grandparents, family members and friends for babysitting to enable you to do this. We used to love having the grandkids for the day—we went on outings with them and enjoyed every minute! If babysitters are in short-supply, do what one couple we met did. They often had to have their weekly date night at home, so they'd get their kids to help set the table, light the candles, even pour the wine, and they'd then leave their parents undisturbed for the rest of the evening. The date night concept is about the sheer joy of being together and doing something that is not child-orientated.

To keep dating your spouse while raising children, you have to be very deliberate. Once it's in the diary, consider it set in stone. Whether it's a movie night, a meal out, or a dinner at home, plan for it, and if an emergency requires you to cancel it, make sure the next one happens without fail. It is so easy to let it slip because being a parent is busy, yet you will find that maintaining your relationship brings great security for each of you. There is nothing that can replace an intimate life within a devoted partnership.

Date nights are a start, yet there are many other things you can incorporate into your daily lives that will enable you to continue building your intimacy at the same time as being parents—things like little gifts that express your love, or notes and text messages that say you love one another or that you appreciate each other's efforts in keeping the family together. Continue to touch, hug, and kiss each other—even in front of the kids. Get creative! Doing these things will not only bless you as a couple but will also demonstrate to your kids what it means to be in a loving relationship.

Lastly, never let your kids separate you. Always be together in how you go about things, discuss everything, and do it openly so that they know they cannot divide you. You are a team. Be careful not to neglect the hidden intimacy that lies behind it all, the private love life that is just for the pair of you, secret and yet demonstrable because your oneness is evident in how you stand shoulder to shoulder in all aspects of life, including parenting. Maintaining these good habits of relationship will enable you to overcome times of conflict, disappointment, fear, uncertainty, and the general busyness of raising a family. That way, when the nest is empty once again, you will still be 'one flesh' as God intended, ready to enjoy a new stage of life together.

13

What if it Goes Wrong?

When we get married, we do so with the intention of cultivating a lifelong partnership. Our hope is to love and be loved. These are normal and healthy desires and goals; a relationship that continues to grow in love and commitment is the ideal. Yet for some couples, it goes wrong and these hopes are shattered. In such situations, the big question many people ask is, *Does God allow divorce?* Or, to put it another way, *If I was to go down the path of divorce, would God approve of it?*

We have already established that God's plan is for male and female to be joined in marriage for life and that what he had joined together, no-one is to separate (Matthew 19:6), so we know that divorce is neither his original design nor something he approves of. Yet we cannot simply leave it there, because we also know that God hates what is wrong, cruel, and unjust, which means sometimes his disapproval of these behaviours will override his objections to divorce. If we both settle in our hearts to walk with God in our marriages and to act according to his will, divorce will most likely never need to be discussed, but we cannot deny that there are some who live with physical and psychological violence, pain, and unfaithfulness for whom there may not, in the end, be any other choice but to end the marriage. It is necessary therefore, for us to consider both the steps that we can take to safeguard our marriages against divorce and what the Bible has to say about the times when divorce is not only permitted, but may also be the necessary step.

SAFEGUARDING OUR MARRIAGES

In our fifty-six years of marriage, Mary and I have been involved with countless couples, both in marriage preparation classes and marriage counselling, as well as in the lives of those who have been under our pastoral care in the churches we have led. And what we have observed is that where both spouses are committed to following God, marriage breakdowns are, in our experience, rare. Of the couples with whom we have been involved in marriage preparation, we are not aware of any that have separated, and of the six couples in our church who married in the same year—including us—only one of them has ended in divorce. The few marriages that we have seen fail in the churches that we have led have usually been precipitated by at least one or both spouses turning their backs on God and his church. There is no doubt that one of the best things we can do to protect our marriages is to strengthen our relationship with the Lord, keeping it our top priority.

Professor Scott Stanley, a researcher and co-director of the Centre for Marital and Family Studies at the University of Denver, found that couples with a vibrant religious faith have more and higher levels of the qualities couples need to avoid divorce. In summary, he wrote:

> "Whether young or old, male or female, low-income or not, those who said that they were more religious reported higher average levels of commitment to their partners, higher levels of marital satisfaction, less thinking and talking about divorce, and lower levels of negative interaction. These patterns held true when controlling for such important variables as income, education, and age at first marriage."

Focus on the Family, who published his findings, agreed that, "Any people who seriously practice a traditional religious faith—be it Christian or other—have a divorce rate markedly lower than the general population."

This gives us much reason to be optimistic about the future of marriage for believers.

In addition to prioritising our faith, we can avoid the need for separation or divorce by putting into practice the lessons and principles we have already shared in this book:

- Commit to your partner
- Respect and honour one other
- Talk and share all the time
- Operate joint finances and be transparent with your money
- Give each other space
- Have regular date nights
- Forgive all the time
- Don't control each other
- Get help when you need it

It goes without saying that for these principles to be effective, they rely on the active participation of both partners. If only one is willing, it can be like hitting a brick wall at every turn. In this case, it is always wise to consider the possibilities. Nobody wants their marriage to fail, but many are in love with an ideal rather than the reality of day-to-day life and are unable or unwilling to see the potential weaknesses in themselves or in the one they love. We must go into marriage with our eyes wide open, preparing and hoping for the best, yet ready to handle the surprises.

For the majority of couples, the problems will be things that can be dealt with if caught early—the clashing of personalities, the frustrations that come from things being different from what was expected, and so on. This is why we highly recommend regular check-ups for your marriage; catching conflicts early on and anticipating problems before they become ingrained is critical. Our experience tells us that if this is done early in married life, many of these problems never get to be longterm issues. Engage trusted mentors that you can talk honestly and openly with. Accountability works! However, there are situations that cannot be considered 'small', nor are they easily dealt with; they go against the core of what marriage is, violating the covenant you have both entered into.

GROUNDS FOR DIVORCE

Statistics tell us that one in four women and one in nine men suffer from some form of domestic violence. Much of this is physical and sexual. However, psychological, mental, financial, and material abuse is also rife. In situations where it goes horribly wrong, where one partner neglects, abuses, betrays, or abandons the other, the question arises: *What do we, as God's people do?* The answer is, we fight! We fight for what is right and do not give up easily. But that does not mean we tolerate behaviour that contravenes our vows to love and cherish one another.

∽

When I was pastoring in London, I met a young man whose wife had left him for another man she'd met at work. As he prayed and fought to get her back, he continued to wear his wedding ring, determined that as long as there was hope, he would keep the promise he had made to love her and be faithful to her. Even though his wife had committed adultery, he still wanted to reconcile. At that point in time, he felt this was God's will for him. He held firm in this belief until she married the man she had left him for and was expecting his baby. He came and told me what had happened, and I advised him to take off his wedding ring and throw it into the river Thames; he was set free from the covenant he had made.

It is difficult to adequately convey in words the pain this man felt at the death of his marriage. He held on and fought as long as there was hope, but when hope was gone, he felt God's release, and in time, he was able to reset his life and move on. He subsequently met and married a wonderful Christian woman with whom he now has four children.

I share his story to encourage you to not give up on your marriage easily—fight while it is still possible to do so—but also to remind you that

God is a God of new beginnings. When there is no hope of restoration for your relationship, hanging on to what cannot be retrieved is fruitless. Allow yourself to reset with God's help and watch what he will do for you.

One of the biggest obstacles Christians face in resetting their life after a relationship breakdown is the erroneous teaching that the church has traditionally held to concerning divorce. We are told that because God hates divorce, no matter what the circumstances, you must stick with your partner or remain celibate for the rest of your life. Many a wife has stayed with her brutally abusive husband because the church has said that she needs to remain faithful regardless of circumstances, and countless numbers of believers have suffered in silence feeling as though it is not acceptable to experience problems in their marriage. To leave is portrayed as somewhat of an unforgiveable sin.

But abuse and violence in any form is never acceptable, and marriage must not be used as an excuse to tolerate and cover it up. In fact, exposure is essential if abuse is to be stopped. This is why the Bible encourages us in James 5:16 to confess our sins to one another and seek prayer. The word 'confess' means 'to acknowledge openly' and has the sense of taking what is in the dark and bringing it into the light. Dark secrets fear the light because light makes them visible, and that is the last thing an abuser wants. Yet it is essential that these things are brought into the light.

If you find yourself in a marriage where infidelity or abuse of any kind has occurred and you do not wish to get a divorce, there are several steps you can take to address what is happening in your relationship. But depending on the nature of the abuse and how entrenched it is, you may first need to seek shelter and support before engaging in any kind of process with your abuser. Violence is never justified or alright in any circumstance and should be reported to the police and charges laid. Be wise and protect yourself from further abuse even as you work to reconcile your relationship.

The first thing you must do when a partner displays abusive behaviour is to set boundaries and to warn your spouse of what will happen should they act in this way again. However, it's important that you are realistic in what you say will happen because you need to be able and willing to follow through if necessary, otherwise you have lost the fight already.

If they continue to disregard the boundaries you have set, then you need to engage a trusted mentor. This may be the couple who did your pre-marital counselling, or you may wish to find someone specialised in dealing with the issues you face. Involving a third party continues the important work of exposing the abuse or infidelity but also preserves a level of privacy for you as a couple, keeping your relationship free from public scrutiny. However, if this, too, fails to work, then you will need to inform your parents, church leaders, and trusted mentors as appropriate. Again, I caution you to exercise wisdom—many people, including church leaders, do not know how to handle such revelations, and may hold to the thinking that you must tolerate such behaviour because you are married. But don't let that put you off. Stand firm, and never accept abuse.

If you find yourself in a situation where it is not safe for your marriage to continue, or you have exhausted all attempts to address the unacceptable dynamics and change has not been possible, or your spouse has been unwilling to restore the relationship, understanding what God has to say about divorce will be critical to your ability to reset and move forward.

In Matthew 19, the religious leaders decided to test Jesus, so they put this question to him: "Is it lawful for a man to divorce his wife for any and every reason?" (v. 3, NIV). Jesus responds to them by restating God's design for marriage:

> *"Haven't you read," he replied, "that at the beginning the Creator 'made them male and female,' and said, 'For this reason a man will leave his father and mother and be united to his wife, and the two will become one flesh'? So they are no longer two, but one flesh. Therefore what God has joined together, let no one separate."*
>
> —vv. 4-6 (NIV)

He then went on to explain that Moses permitted divorce because their hearts were hard but that this was never God's intention. The practice of the day, where a man could give his wife a divorce paper and send her away without reason, was a violation of God's will. Jesus points out that if you do this and marry somebody else you commit adultery—something else that is not God's will. He does, however, go on to say that adultery, or in today's language, 'an affair', is a violation of the marriage covenant and grounds for divorce (v. 9). This is because the covenant relationship between man and wife hinges on them being 'one flesh'. Adultery breaches this union, an act Jesus teaches is so serious it warrants the ending of a marriage. That is not to say reconciliation is never possible, but that if it isn't, the one who has been wronged is released from the obligations of the covenant they entered into.

But adultery is not the only act that breaks the covenant of marriage. In Hebrew, the word translated 'violence' can mean 'something wrong, cruel and unjust'. In Genesis, where God gives his reason for sending the flood, we gain insight into just how strongly God feels about such cruelty and injustice; the violence that filled the earth was the reason he had to destroy it (Genesis 6:13). Similarly, when God was laying out the rules that governed the treatment of a woman who was sold as a servant, we see that if she were chosen as a wife for the master's son, she was to be granted the full rights of a daughter. Should the son take a second wife and in so doing deprive his first wife of food, clothing, and marital rights, she was free to separate and go her own way without penalty (Exodus 21:7-11). This teaches us that abuse can also be grounds for divorce.

While God's design and heart is that marriage would last and that we make every effort to remain together (1 Corinthians 7:10-15), we must be careful to take into account the whole counsel of Scripture and not just one part. When we do so, we will see that as much as God hates divorce, he also hates his children being mistreated. We see this in Malachi when the prophet tells us that God hates a man 'putting his wife away' (that is, divorcing her) but in the same verse, he also says that God hates it when a man perpetuates violence against his wife (Malachi 2:16). God's instructions are very clear: stop mistreating your wife, guard your marriage and remain faithful to her. When a husband—or a wife—is unwilling to repent or take these responsibilities seriously, then the hardness of their heart makes ending the marriage permissible. In these situations, the lavish grace and mercy of God releases us to a new beginning.

Epilogue

I am writing this after having coffee with a friend who shared with me that he has come to understand that there are three 'people' in a marriage: a man, a woman, and an 'us'. As individuals, we have a life outside of our marriage relationship—we go out to work, play sports, and engage in many activities on our own, but we always come back together to a shared life. Whatever we do, we always come back to the 'us'. 'Us' is the place where we can be ourselves with no need for pretence, no need to put up a front or protect ourselves. It's where we are loved, accepted, encouraged, appreciated and strengthened, and it enables us to go out and come back again, and again, and again, confident in the knowledge that we always have that safe intimate place of belonging to return to.

I know this is very idealistic, *but isn't that what we all want? Isn't this what we dream about?* Yes, it may be an ideal, but it is an ideal that we long for, or else why would we have so much literature and so many movies about it? And not only is it our ideal, it's God's. When we come together in marriage, it is to live out God's inbuilt desire to belong, to be loved, to be intimate, to touch, and to be cared for. We do this because it is the way God made us. He created us with the desire for partnership and intimacy.

Mary and I have finished our employment. I am no longer leading a church and we no longer have children dependent on us. Yes, we still serve God and his church, but now there are just us two. Years ago, when I visited an elderly couple in the church I had just become the pastor of, they showed me photos of a Royal Marine, very smart in his uniform, with a beautiful woman and two small children. I realised it was them—they were now well into their eighties, frail, and sitting in what I called their thrones, pushed right up close to each other. I asked them what was important now that they were old and frail? (I'm sure I did not put it quite like that). They replied, "The Lord Jesus and each other are all that matters now." That is what God intends for you, to be in a partnership of equality with your spouse, to be married in his sight, to have made promises to each other that you keep, to love, support and be devoted to one another, and to be intimate for the whole of your lives together.

This 'ideal', this original design, is why I wrote this book. I wanted to help move you from fantasy to reality by giving you the tools to build a successful partnership that will stand the test of time. For a few, this kind of relationship just happens, but for most of us, we will have to work at it because we are all flawed people in some way or another.

Our flaws, or what might be considered our 'negative' ways of coping and processing life, are often formed in our early years through the things that happened to us—through family dynamics, loss, abuse, bullying, school experiences etc. Not only we, but our spouse also has to learn to live with the consequences of our negative conditioning. And this is why I would like to finish this book by sharing one of the greatest insights I can give you. It's a lesson that was hard-won in my own life, but I know that if you can take it on board, it will help your marriage to thrive.

Here, then, is the question I had to grapple with: *Do I know myself? What am I like to live with?* Being able to answer those questions gives you an awareness of what your partner is having to cope with living with you. There is great benefit in seeking to discern early on in your relationship the effect you have on your spouse—it will save you years of unnecessary conflict. We all understand the effect our partner has on us, but it takes revelation to fully understand the impact we ourselves have. Even if it is pointed out to us, we may find it difficult to recognise ourselves and therefore we will reject the picture portrayed. This is largely because, in reality, we just do not know or appreciate what it is like to live with ourselves. We know our motives and intentions, we know that we do not mean to hurt or undermine, but the truth is we do not always come across the way we think we do.

EPILOGUE

Let me use part of my own story to illustrate this. As I've shared, I spent the whole of my school life in boarding school which caused me to become a very fearful boy, lacking confidence. I have always been shy, and left to my own devices I still have a strong tendency to be introverted. But my lack of confidence was more to do with the fear instilled in me than my personality, and it left me unsure that I was capable of what was required of me in various seasons of my life. Mary will tell you that when I became a Christian and entered into church leadership, there were many changes evident in me, yet within myself, I still carried those feelings of inadequacy. But this was not how others saw me. To them, I was a person of authority—wise, considerate, and helpful.

This dichotomy became clear to me some years ago in Bermondsey, South London when our dear friend Chris Brown and I were joining our two churches together to form one new church. We had what we called, a church 'marriage service', which was videoed for posterity. I led the service, and later when it was played back while we were enjoying a celebratory meal, I watched on in fascination. This person looked like me, but I did not recognise the authority with which he led the meeting. He was confident and decisive. Yet internally, I had felt the opposite. *Did this mean that I was pretending, acting even? Was I a hypocrite?* I can assure you I was doing none of those things. I was living with the consequences of my childhood, while at the same time exhibiting to the world my true capability, which God had known when he called me to serve his church.

The person I saw on the screen that day was intriguing to me because I had not understood who I had become in God. I did not truly know myself or how I came across to those around me. My true self was who I was watching, but that identity was being confused by the residual fear of my childhood.

However, our strengths can also be our weaknesses. Translate those same attributes I saw that day into home life and you potentially get a different result. Now, before you get the wrong idea, Mary and I have had a good marriage since we overcame the problems of our early years.

We have grown from strength to strength and enjoy our life together. However, there has been one persistent issue that I have had a lot of trouble understanding. This is expressed by Mary in some thoughts she wrote about how men can demonstrate their love for their wives: *"Flowers? Chocolates? Date Nights? All are very nice and welcome. But these don't bring us to the heart of the matter. What wives need from their husbands is, simply, time. Yes, time to listen, attentively, taking an interest in her views, feelings, and interests that he may not share in."*

I have come to the realisation that there are some aspects of my character that have not been easy to live with. To my thinking, I am harmless, mild, and caring. Yet I see that at home, I, on occasion, demonstrate that I am a man who has strong quick opinions, and what's more, I often deliver those opinions with a measure of authority. What this means in practice is that without intending to do so, I shut down discussion by interrupting and assuming that I know what Mary is going to say, bringing solutions that have not been asked for. *The problem?* I have not understood the effect my quick pronouncements have on Mary and that they can effectively shut down her ability to express herself fully. She has therefore at times not felt like I take an interest in her views and feelings.

It is abundantly true that we need to get to know our life partner's strengths, weaknesses, likes, dislikes in order to support them fully. Yet it is also vital for true harmony that we are aware of our own strengths, weaknesses, likes and dislikes, and the effect they have on the one we love. We might think we know what will bless our partner, *but do we listen in such a way that we can truly understand what supports, blesses, or irritates them?*

To quote Mary again: *"Some years ago, we went to a big meeting about marriage. The well-known speaker shared that one day, he asked his wife what he could do to let her know how much he loved her. He was thinking of flowers and chocolates etc. She looked him in the eye and gave him a shock—she told him, that to show how much he loved her, would he please not leave his shaving hair all around the bathroom sink for her to clean?!"*

EPILOGUE

The things that demonstrate we really hear and know our spouse seldom cost money, but rather are a sacrifice of time and thoughtfulness. As part of my quest to listen to and appreciate Mary, I have discovered the power of a good hug. We have always touched often, making sure we kiss one another goodbye, and hold hands when we go out, but there is something special about stopping and having a really good spontaneous hug. It is a connection that focuses us on each other in a real and tangible way. It makes us both feel better. Somehow, we feel closer to one another—it makes me happy and I'm sure the same is true for Mary. I do not fully understand why it has this effect, but it seems to generate a sense of togetherness. I love it!

A good marriage is a great thing and is worth every effort you invest into it. Always remember the promises you made to each other when you married; keep them in mind and be faithful to them all the days you are together.

As I put these last words on paper Mary and I have just had our fifty-sixth wedding anniversary. We have had to work on our marriage. It has not always been easy but it has, in the fullness of time, been very beneficial and it is in good shape for whatever years we have left. Mary and I pray that God will bless your own togetherness abundantly and that you will truly find the oneness which is at the heart of God's design for marriage. May all that you undertake together be fruitful as you remember that at the centre of your life is an 'us'.

> *"'For this reason a man will leave his father and mother and be united to his wife, and the two will become one flesh.' So they are no longer two, but one flesh. Therefore what God has joined together, let no one separate."*
> —MATTHEW 19:5-6 (NIV)

Appendix

MARRIAGE HEALTH INDICATOR

Husband's Name: _____

Date: _____

Read each of the following statements and ask yourself, "Is this true of my marriage relationship?"

Give each question a score on the scale below:

3	2	1	0
Completely true			**Not true at all**

1	I am listened to	
2	We pray regularly together	
3	I enjoy making love	
4	I am happy with the way we use our money	
5	I feel listened to when decisions have to be made	
6	I love my partner touching me	
7	My viewpoint is valued	
8	We pray together about most things	
9	We make love regularly enough for me	

10	We budget our finances together	
11	I feel I am an equal in my marriage	
12	We still kiss often	
13	I feel accepted by my partner	
14	It matters to me that we pray together regularly	
15	My needs are met when we make love	
16	I know when my partner is going to buy something (apart from presents for me)	
17	My input is appreciated	
18	We have regular special times together	
19	I contribute a lot to the relationship	
20	I feel comfortable when praying together	
21	I can communicate when I want to make love	
22	I feel I am provided for in my day-to-day personal financial requirements	
23	My partner respects me	
24	I get cuddled enough	
25	I feel appreciated by my partner	
26	I am content with our praying together	
27	My partner satisfies me when we make love	
28	We discuss the use of our money	
29	I feel I am important in my marriage	
30	I miss my partner when we are apart	
31	My views are heard and considered	
32	Disagreements or arguments end up with us praying together	
33	I enjoy making love because my partner meets my needs	
34	We don't have 'his and hers' money - our money is ours	
35	I can be myself in our marriage	
36	We spend time doing things together	
37	My perspectives are important on issues that need discussion and decision	
38	When facing something new or making decisions we pray about it	

APPENDIX

39	I come to a climax when we make love	
40	Our finances are under control	
41	My partner is interested in my life outside the marriage	
42	I love spending time with my partner	
43	My point of view is listened to	
44	When I'm down my partner prays for me	
45	My partner has a good understanding of my sexual desires	
46	We both like to give and help others in more need than ourselves	
47	We have a real partnership in our marriage	
48	My partner shows her love for me by what she does	

Enter your score into the chart below, being careful to enter your score against the relevant question number (e.g. score for question 1 in Box 1 and so on). Then add up your ratings from left to right and enter the totals under the column headed 'total'. (Each line relates to a different aspect of your marriage).

								Total	
1	7	13	19	25	31	37	43		Communication
2	8	14	20	26	32	38	44		Prayer
3	9	15	21	27	33	39	45		Sex
4	10	16	22	28	34	40	46		Money
5	11	17	23	29	35	41	47		Personal Contentment
6	12	18	24	30	36	42	48		Non-sexual Affection

The highest scores reflect the strongest aspects of your marriage and the lowest the weakest.

Remember, this is an indicator! Each weakness should be discussed and prayed about together and we would highly recommend the counsel of a third party. Remember, you are not looking for perfection, but seeking to understand weaknesses in your marriage and how you can strengthen those weaknesses.

You can look at the individual questions and discuss your scores and why you scored it the way you did. Any individual score can be discarded if the statement is irrelevant to you both.

MARRIAGE HEALTH INDICATOR

Wife's Name: _____

Date: _____

Read each of the following statements and ask yourself, "Is this true of my marriage relationship?"

Give each question a score on the scale below:

         3   2   1   0

Completely true   **Not true at all**

1	I am listened to	
2	We pray regularly together	
3	I enjoy making love	
4	I am happy with the way we use our money	
5	I feel listened to when decisions have to be made	
6	I love my partner touching me	
7	My viewpoint is valued	
8	We pray together about most things	
9	We make love regularly enough for me	
10	We budget our finances together	
11	I feel I am an equal in my marriage	
12	We still kiss often	
13	I feel accepted by my partner	
14	It matters to me that we pray together regularly	
15	My needs are met when we make love	

16	I know when my partner is going to buy something (apart from presents for me)	
17	My input is appreciated	
18	We have regular special times together	
19	I contribute a lot to the relationship	
20	I feel comfortable when praying together	
21	I can communicate when I want to make love	
22	I feel I am provided for in my day-to-day personal financial requirements	
23	My partner respects me	
24	I get cuddled enough	
25	I feel appreciated by my partner	
26	I am content with our praying together	
27	My partner satisfies me when we make love	
28	We discuss the use of our money	
29	I feel I am important in my marriage	
30	I miss my partner when we are apart	
31	My views are heard and considered	
32	Disagreements or arguments end up with us praying together	
33	I enjoy making love because my partner meets my needs	
34	We don't have 'his and hers' money - our money is ours	
35	I can be myself in our marriage	
36	We spend time doing things together	
37	My perspectives are important on issues that need discussion and decision	
38	When facing something new or making decisions we pray about it	
39	I come to a climax when we make love	
40	Our finances are under control	
41	My partner is interested in my life outside the marriage	
42	I love spending time with my partner	
43	My point of view is listened to	
44	When I'm down my partner prays for me	
45	My partner has a good understanding of my sexual desires	

APPENDIX

46	We both like to give and help others in more need than ourselves	
47	We have a real partnership in our marriage	
48	My partner shows his love for me by what he does	

Enter your score into the chart below, being careful to enter your score against the relevant question number (e.g. score for question 1 in Box 1 and so on). Then add up your ratings from left to right and enter the totals under the column headed 'total'. (Each line relates to a different aspect of your marriage).

								Total	
1	7	13	19	25	31	37	43		Communication
2	8	14	20	26	32	38	44		Prayer
3	9	15	21	27	33	39	45		Sex
4	10	16	22	28	34	40	46		Money
5	11	17	23	29	35	41	47		Personal Contentment
6	12	18	24	30	36	42	48		Non-sexual Affection

The highest scores reflect the strongest aspects of your marriage and the lowest the weakest.

Remember, this is an indicator! Each weakness should be discussed and prayed about together and we would highly recommend the counsel of a third party. Remember, you are not looking for perfection, but seeking to understand weaknesses in your marriage and how you can strengthen those weaknesses.

You can look at the individual questions and discuss your scores and why you scored it the way you did. Any individual score can be discarded if the statement is irrelevant to you both.

Recommended Ministries and Resources

INTIMACY

Intended for pleasure, by Ed and Gaye Wheat

Love Life for Every Married Couple, by Ed Wheat

A Touch of Love, by John and Janet Houghton

Men are from Mars, Women are from Venus, by John Gray

Marriage365.com

Sex Awakened, by Renee Yam

FINANCES

Christians Against Poverty (CAP)

Youneedabudget.com

Money and the Prosperous Soul, by Stephen K. De Silva

Poverty, Riches and Wealth, by Kris Vallotton

COMMUNICATION

Now You're Speaking My Language, by Gary Chapman

Communication in Marriage, by Marcus and Ashley Kusi

Acknowledgements

Mary, your encouragement to not only start but to persevere in the writing of this book has been outstanding. I have often wanted to give up, but you have always reminded me that it is God who has prompted me to record all the lessons we have learned—both from our own experience and that of the couples we have together prepared for marriage or helped along the way. I may have written this book, but you have been my partner in it all. What's more, you have checked every word and every story, then read it all again and again. It is not only your help in this project that I thank you for, but for the fifty-six years we have been partners in this life. I love you more than I ever did and look forward to whatever years we still have together.

My thanks also go to **my family** who have put up with me trying out my concepts and insights, not just once or twice, but over and over again. Your encouragement is beyond measure. I love you all and am so glad you are a part of our lives. Catherine, our daughter-in-law, read the manuscript and was a great help with her encouragement and suggestions. Much love to all my wonderful family. I love each one of you more than words can ever express.

The completion of this project would not have been possible without Anya McKee, Aimée Walker, and the entire team at **Torn Curtain Publishing**. I am so glad I picked up one of your books and got in touch. From the moment you read the draft manuscript, you have encouraged, cajoled (in a good way) and helped me complete this project.

Lastly, to all **my friends** who have put up with me sharing my insights on marriage, which knowing me I have repeated over and over again. Thank you.

www.ingramcontent.com/pod-product-compliance
Lightning Source LLC
Chambersburg PA
CBHW022016290426
44109CB00015B/1195